Praise for
SEARCHING FOR GOD

"*Searching for God* not only offers an inspiring, emotional insight to the author's journey to and through Islam, it beautifully maps out Islamic principles in an understandable and relatable way. Truly a five-star read!"
—**Ameena Blake**, Muslim scholar, UK

"A story of a Christian who always carried Islam – unknowingly – in her heart until she finally discovered it, then artistically crafted her experience with a feather. Rarely does a book touch my heart and inspire me like that."
—**Fadel Soliman,** Founder, Bridges Foundation

"... a heartfelt reflection on a personal journey to Islam, filled with insights expressed with refreshing clarity. Teresa pens an invaluable narrative—an inspiring beacon for those on the path to discovering the beauty of Islam and the religion's unique quality of elevating the seemingly mundane to the sacred. *Searching for God* is a love letter written for all seekers but especially for those looking for a way to imbue meaning and purpose into every aspect of life."
—**Sondos Kholaki**, author of *Musings of a Muslim Chaplain*

"... such a friendly read! The inspirational reflections shared in this memoir lead one to ponder deeply on how we are fellow travelers on this journey we call life."
—**Marilu**, Founder of The Revert Channel

"Dr. Teresa Lesher takes the reader on a fascinating journey inside her life as an American convert to Islam who has lived in Kuwait for more than 40 years. She shares profound, thought-provoking lessons she's

learned about life, love, Islam, culture, and God, amongst many other things. Written by a beautiful soul who has much wisdom to share and has generously done so in this unique memoir. This is a wonderful, must-read for anyone interested in the lived experience of Islam in the life of a practicing Muslim, navigating life within a cross-cultural context, making meaning out of life, cultivating inner peace and well-being, and developing a relationship with God."
—**Carrie M. York**, PhD, Founder and President
The Alkaram Institute www.alkaraminstitute.org

"*Searching for God, Finding Love* is a profound account of the author's soul-searching spiritual journey and her providential encounter with Islam as a living religion. Each page is full of sincere and heartfelt discovery of God's Presence and a way of embodying this discovery in a Prophetically virtuous manner. The author, Dr. Teresa Lesher, who resides in Kuwait, has successfully distilled a meaningfully lived life through the practical wisdom of the Qur'an and the Sunnah of the Prophet Muhammad (s). There are many reflections that are quite engaging and relevant to the psycho-spiritual challenges that contemporary seekers of all faiths or wisdom traditions face. This inspiring life story is full of applied and beneficial knowledge for the seeker of truth interested in one of the world's fastest-growing religions. Highly recommended for those who are interested in a timely example of bridging the challenges and opportunities found in modern culture with the timeless values and spirit of Islam."
—**Hasan Awan**, M.D. Al-Qadiri-Shadhili
Founder of Hudur Institute, www.hudur.org

"In the following pages, you are about to embark on a journey unlike any other—a journey through a life lived with remarkable zest and unyielding passion. This autobiography isn't just a chronicle of events; it's a living manual that vividly demonstrates how Islam is as much a lifestyle as it is a religion, offering a unique perspective on how faith can guide and enrich every aspect of life.

"Teresa, a modern-day adventurer with roots as deep and diverse as the cultures she's explored, invites you into a world many dare not venture. Her writing uncovers the uncharted territories of both the physical world and the human soul. Her story is a testament to living a fantastic life off the beaten path, where conventions are challenged and discoveries are plenty.

"At the heart of this book is a tale of love—a love for people, for culture, for the divine, and, most importantly, for life itself. Through Teresa's eyes, you'll witness the beauty and depth found within Islam for those who seek it.

"This autobiography is essential reading for anyone looking for guidance through life's complexities. It doesn't offer easy answers but shares wisdom from a life lived fully and fearlessly, reflecting the joys, challenges, and triumphs of a journey led by faith, curiosity, and unrelenting passion.

"As you turn these pages, prepare to be transported, inspired, and changed. This book is not just about a life lived, but also a guide on the art of living."

—**Ronny Engen**, Norway, Entrepreneur and Philanthropist

"*Searching for God, Finding Love* takes the reader on an intimate human journey. With wisdom learned from life and from the Quran, Lesher allows the reader to pause and reflect. The stories, poems, and essays in this book can be shared with Muslim friends and friends of other faiths. They bring us all together in the experience of loving God and remind us to slow down and pay attention to all the beauty we are given on our own paths.

"Pour yourself a pot of hot tea, add a drop of milk, and settle in to spend an afternoon with the author. She will become your friend, and help you to refocus and return to the path of Divine discovery."

—**Dr. Tamara Gray**

Executive Director & Chief Spirituality Officer – Rabata

"When I've participated in interfaith dialogue or worked with Muslim kids, I've found that their biggest interest can be summed up in the question, 'What does it feel like to be a Muslim?' And that's a hard question to answer. It's about describing personal faith, not explaining the five pillars or all the other topics taught in typical Islamic school curricula. Searching for God, Finding Love, with its short descriptive stories from the life of a Muslim woman, illustrates those deep feelings

of growing in faith far better than I've ever been able to express myself. I'm very grateful to the author for sharing her experiences."
—**Norma Tarazi,** author of *Child in Islam and Practical Parenting for Muslims*

SEARCHING FOR GOD

Finding Love

Teresa Lesher

TUGHRA
BOOKS

*At last I have arrived
at the beginning*

Published by Tughra Books

335 Clifton Ave.

Clifton, NJ, 07011, USA

www.tughrabooks.com

ISBN: 978-1-59784-959-3

Ebook: 978-1-59784-995-1

Library of Congress Cataloging-in-Publication Data

Names: Lesher, Teresa, author.
Title: Searching for God, finding love / Teresa Lesher.
Description: Clifton : Tughra Books, 2024.
Identifiers: LCCN 2023041863 (print) | LCCN 2023041864 (ebook) | ISBN
    9781597849593 (hardcover) | ISBN 9781597849951 (ebook)
Subjects: LCSH: God (Islam) | God (Islam)--Love. | Faith (Islam)
Classification: LCC BP166.2 .L475 2024 (print) | LCC BP166.2 (ebook) |
    DDC 297.2/11--dc23/eng/20230918
LC record available at https://lccn.loc.gov/2023041863
LC ebook record available at https://lccn.loc.gov/2023041864

Printed in Canada

CONTENTS

3. DEVOTION 93

Notes from the Author

Throughout this book, references are made to verses from the Quran. There is one version of the Quran in Arabic, a widely available volume that has remained unchanged since its transcription 1450 years ago. However, there are many translations of the Quran in English and most major languages, each with merits and shortcomings. I have mainly used the popular translation of the Quran by Saheeh International, as it offers a nearly word-for-word translation that avoids literary embellishments; however, I must emphasize that it is impossible to either translate the layered and nuanced meaning of the Arabic scripture, or capture the rhythm and rhyme of the verses. The translation in English, therefore, is an approximation of the basic meaning, the fullness of which is challenging to grasp even in Arabic. In this book, the translations of verses from the Quran are referenced with parentheses to indicate (chapter:verse).

The terms God and Allah are used interchangeably throughout this book. "Allah" is an Arabic word that literally means "the God" and is the Creator's proper name by which He introduces Himself in the Quran. Both Arabic speaking Christians and Muslims refer to God the Creator as Allah, the name that is present in both the Arabic Christian Bible and the Arabic Quran. The word Allah is unique in the sense that, unlike the word "god," it cannot be rendered generic, plural, masculine or feminine, which is a reflection of the reality of the Divine.

Muslims customarily follow mention of the Prophet Muhammad with the salutation "may the peace and blessings of God be upon him." However, to keep the flow of the text undisturbed, and to adhere to a style comfortable to the reader, I have omitted the salutation within the text, but offer it here: *May the peace and blessings of God be upon His messenger and servant, Muhammad son of Abdullah, amen.*

Finally, although I have adhered to the literal translation of pronouns in Quranic verses, which are almost always masculine, I would like to remind the reader that masculine and plural pronouns in the Quran usually include the feminine as well. Consider this verse from the Knowing and Subtle Creator: *"Whoever does righteousness, whether male or female, while he is a believer – We will surely cause him to live a good life, and We will surely give them their reward according to the best of what they used to do"* (16:97).

Introduction

One of my earliest memories is of contemplating God. I was a freckle-faced girl of five, sitting quietly in catechism class when the teacher casually said, "God is bigger than everything." The words hit me like a blast force. The classroom disappeared, the teacher's voice muted, and I gasped at the revelation. Bigger than the tallest tree in the yard? Bigger than a mountain? Bigger than the world? The enormity of God impressed me, but I couldn't help wondering, "If He is bigger than anything, where is He?"

Since then, I have been searching for God. Growing up Catholic, I found him in church on Sundays. As a born-again teenager, I found Him in Jesus. As a Muslim, I found Him in daily prayers and annual fasting. Never satisfied, I wanted more. I wanted to experience God in every moment and capture that which is unmistakably divine, and then internalize it, making it mine. My search for God has been a quest for both vitality and transcendence, for both certainty and mystery, for meaning and integrity, and mostly for inner peace and a life where love prevails.

The journey has been long and the discoveries sometimes elusive. It has been a journey like anyone's walk through life, but I have spent much of it searching with my inner eye for something beyond the apparent, for something transcendent. It has been a journey to the other side of the world, to the land of prophets who beckon me and inform my choices. And it has been a journey to my innermost self where I dissect issues that fascinate me and confront questions that baffle me.

This book, written over a period of several years, is a journey of self-discovery and religious identity. It searches for God, the purpose of life and how to live well. It delves into concepts such as freedom, trust, and love. It explores what it means to be human, and what it means to be a Muslim.

The most important guide in this journey has been the Quran, considered by Muslims as the direct, unadulterated speech of God, sent from the heavens to all mankind, as much a message for its conduit, Prophet Muhammad, as it is for every woman and man alive today. It is the voice that has directed me in my search for God, shaping my thoughts and deeds along the way.

This book is a collection of essays about my life, about those who have made me who I am, about elating moments, hard times and hope. It is a record of my exploration of what it means, to me, to be a Muslim, and of my journey of study, contemplation, practice, soul-searching and longing. I hope it will be a worthwhile perspective for others who are also searching for God.

THE JOURNEY

Not so long ago
I journeyed in the desert
And guess what I found?
Come with me
Come with me.

I came upon a vision
Pure and radiant light
Wondrous to behold
Irresistible, indescribable.
And I
Unable to hold the light
Cannot bring you some
So come with me
Come with me.

I came upon a book
Words of warning and wisdom
Full of hope and love
Light on the tongue and ear
Residing in the heart so clear.

And yet,
Its language is unknown to you.
Let me help you
Come with me.

I came upon a spring
Absolute grace, a peaceful place.
Its water granted life to me
Nourishing and cleansing me.
And you
Cannot really live
Without what it gives.
So come with me
Come with me.

There is a man
Who can show you all of these
Would you like to meet him?
Come with me
Come with me.

1

DIRECTION

1

DIRECTION

When my granddaughter Soraya was a baby, I would watch her as she slept peacefully, and wonder who she would become.

Many things would shape her – parents, culture, education – setting her in a general direction on a predictable path. Like Soraya, all of us are born into particular circumstances, with both advantages and challenges that put an indelible mark on our identities, shaping and influencing who we are. But it does not limit who we can become. We are constantly exposed to influences on our path in life, and who we finally become is a result of how we concede to be shaped by those influences.

No matter the circumstances of our early lives, we are not prevented from searching for God and His guidance; in fact, it seems to be a most natural quest. This section explores factors that have made me who I am as well as the influencers that shape who I want to be, and lead me in my search for God. It describes some of the mentors, teachers, role models and guides that have impacted me and provided direction along the way.

What are some of the forces that have shaped your identity? What are some of the influences that you have allowed to shape your destiny?

Fallen Gods

"What do you want to be when you grow up?" my third-grade teacher asked me. "I want to be just like Mommy," I said, for she was perfect. Or so I thought, until I realized, like all children do, that she wasn't. Neither was my father. They were the first of the fallen gods.

I turned to myself, the only one I could control or change and became the best I could be. Dean's list, class president, most valuable player, the "most likely to succeed." I saw the world and all its possibilities, yet I found it empty. And worse, my innermost self was void and the significance of anything I had done or hoped to do escaped me. Happiness was not something I could find alone.

Then I met him. He touched my heart and the world was right again. Ecstasy, then bliss, then contentment then comfort. There had to be more.

So she was born. As the product of that perfect love, she was the perfection I sought. All my love and energy were poured on her. She filled me with pride and hope and love, and my life was complete. Until another was born.

While I sought perfect love unaccompanied, I found it in two, or rather three, or maybe more. Love was the group. Generosity and kindness to one another, comfort and satisfaction in the crowd. But at times that love was selective and self-serving.

Unable to find what I sought in others, I turned to *things*. Bigger, better, more and faster. Then I lost my gold bracelet—a prized yet insignificant thing—and through the tears I saw how ugly it had all become. Promises of pleasure and happiness would never be fulfilled.

I looked at nature, the purest of gifts. Autumn's leaves. The first snowfall. Lilacs in spring. Summer twilight and lightning bugs. But life took me elsewhere, where autumn, snowfall, lilacs, and lightning bugs were reduced to mere memories.

And so I stood alone, abandoned, stripped of all my gods, lonely and longing for a true God, a worthy, absolute, ineffable god. And I heard a gentle whisper, "Go back to your fallen gods and love them for My sake and in My service. Hold hands and walk towards Me. Come altogether in search of Me."

And so I begin my journey. For strength I depend on Him, the Giver of all bounties, the Source of all good, the Guide and Patient One.

I am sure this God will not fail me.

The "Other"

Mark Twain said, "Travel is fatal to prejudice, bigotry, and narrow-mindedness, and many of our people need it sorely on these accounts. Broad, wholesome, charitable views of men and things cannot be acquired by vegetating in one little corner of the earth all one's lifetime." I am the first to admit that when I stay too long in my "little corner of the earth," my worldview narrows and my sense of self expands so that my own customs, beliefs, and purpose overshadow others'. When I move beyond my space and into the space of others, and when I interact with people of different lifestyles, religions, and outlooks, I always come home a better person. I see our similarities – our aspirations, our virtues, our concerns – and I hope they have seen the same by interacting with me.

Meaningful interaction with others is sorely lacking in our world, where we seem increasingly divided and polarized into "us" and "them." To overcome this, we must be willing to share parts of ourselves and to try to understand the experiences of others. Once we connect with others in common threads of knowledge and experience, we can begin to weave them together into a tapestry of understanding and respect. Indeed, we should purposefully intertwine until each of us is recognized as part of a colorful and durable cloth called humanity.

The Quran says that God created "*you from male and female and made you peoples and tribes that you may know one another*" (49:13) and that in "*the diversity of your languages and your colors... are signs for those of knowledge*" (30:22). Our differences, therefore, are a reason to learn about each other and, more importantly, to *know* one another. So I must ask myself, How can I *know* about someone who is different from me? I may think I know another because I observe her from a distance, I watch the news, I travel, I read. But until I hear directly from the "other" I cannot really know her, what she believes, what she thinks, what she feels – *who she is*.

Getting to know one another requires dialogue, and dialogue requires people willing to share their stories. We should not allow others to tell our stories. I can only really know you by hearing your narrative in your own words, and you can only know me by hearing my narrative in my own words. But we must look beyond the surface, the incidental, the commonplace – even the contradictions. We must open our hearts and minds to what makes us both unique and the same. We may find that we have much in common. We will certainly find shared experiences, aspirations and deepest emotions. We may discover, in our inner heart, parts of ourselves in each other. And when I know others as I know myself, I can treat others as I would like to be treated, and I can love for others what I love for myself.

Is that not what all great religions ask of us?

Living Among Muslims

Kuwait has been my home for most of my adult life. Married to a lifetime resident of Kuwait, I arrived in the 1980s when it was a quaint desert town with a family-focused atmosphere, and I was a young mother from a sheltered background. I naturally struggled with language and culture – for many years, in fact – feeling confused and off-balance until I eventually figured out, consciously and subconsciously, how to handle myself and my cross-cultural relationships with others. In the years since I first arrived, I have learned much about the Middle East, about myself and about life in general. But some of the most valuable lessons have come from ordinary people, random acquaintances and passersby.

In a country that has a high highway mortality rate I learned about driving. I learned about defensive driving, about the importance of wearing my seatbelt, about focusing on getting to my destination in one piece, and about relaxing so I don't add to the recklessness on the street. And one day I discovered the heart of the matter as I drove past the scene of an accident in the middle of an intersection. An Arab man, his car having been rear-ended by another car, leapt out and rushed towards the other driver who sat stunned behind the steering wheel. He swung open her car door and exclaimed, "Are you alright? I'm so worried about you!" In that single moment, I learned something more valuable than any book about driving could have taught me. Foregoing the reactive feelings of anger, fear and loss, a driver in a character-revealing moment chose empathy, concern, and forgiveness. From his words, which floated through my car window – faceless, nameless – I learned how to drive in Kuwait.

Other lessons came from people and names more familiar, like Khalid and Farida, who taught me about neighbors. Coming from a place where things are labeled as "mine" and "theirs," I am accustomed to placing invisible lines around property, belongings and relationships. Even my glance stays in my own yard. But our neighbors Khalid and Farida destroyed my lines and demolished my divisive paradigm. Early in the morning she knocked on my door, her cheerful voice calling "ya ahl al-bayt!" *oh people of the house!* to bring some fresh-baked bread. At noon, noticing our guests arriving one carload at a time, Khalid stopped by to offer the use of his lawn which partially joined with ours. "And take our chairs and grill... anything you need is yours... promise us you'll use it." The next day, when their multitudes of family members gathered in a house no bigger than ours, they brought us by the arm to meet them, and filled us with food and drink beyond our usual capacity. Accustomed to life in the West, I used to pull in the driveway quietly, keep the curtains pulled, and cook for few. But Khalid and Farida, their arms outstretched, their hearts and hands wide open, showed me what a neighbor should be – a builder of relationships, not fences, whose paradigm is inclusive, not singular.

But meeting Kuwaitis is not always easy, since they are reserved in public and perhaps wary, understandably, of us foreigners who outnumber them two to one. Encounters with them are short and often frustrating, as they take liberties we feel they don't deserve – their country or not – having our own sense of entitlement and cultural perspective of propriety. I learned to seize opportunities for what little interaction I may have with local citizens. One day as I was giving my order at Naif Restaurant – grilled chicken, tabouli, deluxe hummus dip – the Kuwaiti man beside me (not behind me) interrupted to ask the cashier how "deluxe" is different from regular hummus dip. My first reaction was to reclaim my position and not allow the cashier to attend to another customer before finishing my order. But I hesitated and suddenly found myself engaged in their conversation about the merits of fresh herbs in hummus. Camaraderie replaced resentment and I realized that I almost lost a chance for a rare occurrence these days: live human interaction with the "other." I walked away with a feeling of satisfaction that had little to do with grilled chicken. These moments of friendly interaction, devoid of resentment or a sense of entitlement, rewarded me with a feeling of acceptance and belonging. I was part of a community.

Food seems to be one of our greatest common denominators. At the grocery store I asked a Kuwaiti woman about the use of a spice, as I was about to try a local recipe. She attempted to explain in broken English (I don't speak *her* language) and then she enthusiastically offered, "Come home with me now and I'll show you how to make it!" Astonished, I could only admire her for offering to give me some of her time – who can spare any time these days? She taught me that time is never wasted when building relationships.

Of course, not everyone is that eager to help others. Sometimes I find bored employees shirking their responsibilities or not even knowing what they are. They direct me from one office to another for information, stamps, and signatures, as if trying to prove how professional they are, yet exposing instead their inefficiency and disorganization. While I anticipate and point out their shortcomings, they believe in and expect my virtues. For example, when I couldn't decide between three carpets under consideration, the Irani carpet salesman urged me to "take them all home and try each one with your furniture. Tomorrow you can decide." He didn't take any money, phone number or ID card. Never have I been so concerned about returning a loan! And when a corner grocer didn't have change for a 20 KD bill, he said, "No problem, bring the money next time you pass by" and wouldn't allow me to return the groceries to the shelf. They so easily trusted a foreigner and stranger, bringing out my best qualities. Now I can't help but wonder how they would react if I also stopped doubting them and believed in their best intentions and effort. Although I may never fully understand the culture of the Arabs, I do know that their ideals and assumptions are generous and optimistic.

I can't thank all the people who have impacted my life in Kuwait, such as the young Arab who accompanied me once on a drive through the desert. "It's so beautiful!" he exclaimed as he gazed across the bleak, beige landscape. It took me years to understand what he meant by what I thought at the time was an absurd statement. The desert means freedom! It is freedom from all things manmade – things that block the horizon and break the silence – and from things that distract us from the wisdom that we gain only from looking inwards and upwards. My time in the scorched desert of Kuwait has made me keenly aware of my dependence on others for survival, for companionship, for growth, and for gentleness in a harsh world.

I know I have changed for the better because of the people of Kuwait. And I sometimes wonder what, if anything, they have learned from me. I hope I have given a fraction of what I have gained. I hope that I have not been the only beneficiary of my life among Muslims in Kuwait.

My Story

Most stories begin when we are born. And surely there is significance in the circumstances, people and events of our birth and childhood, but there are specific major events in our lives that fundamentally change us. For me, the most significant event in my life was deciding to be a Muslim, and so my story begins with the events leading up to that decision.

Having just started college in a town away from home, I felt a sense of independence and new beginnings. Being what I considered a devout Christian, I also had to find a new church in the area, so I decided to explore the options, even those outside of my denomination. I realized that I was free to choose the practice that suited me best. This gave me a sense of empowerment and self-determination.

Meanwhile, I took a course in logic, thinking it would be an easy A. The subject matter fascinated me. For those who are unfamiliar with logic as an academic subject, it is concerned with the principles governing the validity of arguments and correct reasoning. We explored the concepts of premises, assumptions, propositions, contradictions, proofs, deduction, induction, and so forth. During this time I was exposed to examples of faulty logic and became more aware of how people think and present their arguments. (I got an A, but it wasn't as easy as I thought!)

In my spare time, I participated in the International Student Association on campus, where I had the opportunity to meet students from all over the world. I became close friends with several foreign students, and we would often compare our languages, cultures, and religions. Apart from the fun we had, I realized that the way I was raised – with my cultural traditions, customs and assumptions – was not necessarily the standard or the model. There were many other ways, and they were just as viable as my own, at least to someone.

Eventually, one of the students in the association started attending church with me and seemed particularly interested in Christianity. Being a Muslim, he had many questions about Christianity, and I found myself having to explain my beliefs and practices to someone with little knowledge of the subject. It's not as easy as I thought it would be. Being raised a Christian among other Christians, I never had to explain or defend my faith, since we just took it for granted. I found it difficult to explain my beliefs, which I realized I had accepted without much question. I often heard myself saying things that sounded illogical – now that I understood the basics of logic – such as the notion of transferring sin from one person to another. I was extremely frustrated one day after trying to explain the trinity, which my friend just couldn't grasp, and was becoming increasingly embarrassed by the logical complexity of my faith. So, to turn the tables, I asked him, "So what do you believe?"

These four experiences were like paths that converged at a crossroads. At that crossroads, I first heard about Islam. Islam was simple: there is one God who created everything; He expects us to recognize Him and worship Him exclusively; He provided guidelines for our lives, which, if followed, will lead to success. Islam was logical: there is only one god, so no one else is God; He is unlike His creation who are dependent and mortal; if God is perfect, He cannot be unjust. Islam also supported my feelings of empowerment and responsibility: our lives have purpose; we are created good and free of sin; we are eventually answerable for our deeds and words. I looked at Islam as a way of life to assess its intrinsic worth and validity. I found its principles sound, its prescriptions wholesome, its prohibitions warranted, its flexibility necessary for our complex lives, and its promise of Paradise enticing.

I stood at the crossroads and considered the choices I had. I could deny Islam, reject it, and try to forget it, knowing that it would demand a change in lifestyle from me. Or I could acknowledge, accept and affirm it, even though admitting its simple truth would necessitate rejecting some of my Christian beliefs, a few of which I had come to view as unjust or illogical. Would God expect me to believe something against justice and logic?

The choice was mine alone; as the Quran says, "*Whoever wills – let him believe! And whoever wills – let him disbelieve!*" (18:29). The principle that every soul will bear responsibility for its own deeds, meaning that no one can pay for my sins, nagged at me. What if it's true? I wondered. If God is just, it is certainly true. And what would I stand to lose if I accepted Islam? It doesn't ask me for anything but sincere worship, good work, modesty and kindness. Even if there was no final reward for living as a Muslim, I had absolutely nothing to lose by worshiping my Creator exclusively and being the best person I could be. If the Quran's promises were indeed true, I had everything to gain both in this life and the next. So what was stopping me from becoming a Muslim? Nothing, I decided. From the crossroads, I moved forward and the journey ever since has been utterly amazing.

To most people, I seem average enough – raising a family, holding a job, passing through the ordinary stages of life. But my life as a Muslim is indescribably rich. It is one of clarity, serenity, assuredness and closeness to the wellspring of goodness. God promised that "*Whoever does righteousness, whether male or female, while he is a believer – We will surely cause him to live a good life, and We will surely give them their reward according to the best of what they used to do*" (16:97). God's promise for this life has held true, making me absolutely sure that I took the right decision when the circumstances of my life converged at the crossroads of Islam.

My Mothers

I have been fortunate to have known two amazing women in my life – my mother and my mother-in-law. The circumstances of their lives were very different, but their legacies are identical. My mother was born in Europe at the start of World War II, and, after a traumatic childhood, immigrated to the United States as a young bride. Between moving from city to city in an unstable marriage, she gave birth to six children in rapid succession. Unable to cope with the demands of family life, my father left without a trace, leaving my mother to raise us alone. After crying for a week straight, she pulled herself together and did everything she could to keep us fed, clothed and, most importantly, together.

My mother-in-law had the privilege of attending nursing school before she married a schoolteacher. She also suffered some instability in her marriage due to her husband being frequently imprisoned for political activism against both the British occupation of Egypt and the military regime that followed. With three young children, they moved to Kuwait, had a fourth child and built a life there that would span half a century. During those years, she was a homemaker while her husband dedicated his life to education – first as a school principal, and eventually as director of the many national vocational education institutes that he established. Her home was a hub for a growing extended family, receiving guests every single night of the week for food and conversation. She did everything she could to keep the whole family fed, cared for and, most importantly, together.

My siblings and I grew up and, one by one, left my mother's house. She remarried, and could have moved on to build a new life with her husband, without the drama of young adults. But she continued to make her children the center of her life as she welcomed us back home, babysat the grandkids, flew in for birthdays and graduation ceremonies, and organized reunions. She learned social media to keep in touch, called often, and passed the phone around to keep us all connected.

My mother-in-law, too, gave above and beyond her maternal duty, taking in siblings, parents, nieces and others in need of a home. She hosted a weekly meal for her children and their families, a feast laden with delicacies she knew working mothers had no time to cook.

She welcomed her grown children home, babysat grandkids, and was the physical link among a dozen or more families who, because of her, stayed connected.

My mothers don't have résumés, nor have they held prestigious positions in the community. But Prophet Muhammad praised them, saying, "Paradise is at the feet of mothers." The selflessness of their lives has impacted their communities in constructive, if subtle, ways. For their quiet sacrifices they deserve my profound gratitude and generous attention.

A man asked Prophet Muhammad, "Who among the people is most deserving of my kindest companionship?" He replied, "Your mother." The man asked, "Who is next?" The Prophet said, "Next is your mother." He asked again, "Who is next?" The Prophet said, "Again, it is your mother." Persisting, the man asked, "Who is next?" Then, the Prophet said, "Next is your father."[1] While the father's importance in the family cannot be underestimated, the mother is the heartbeat of the home, her influence beyond calculation.

My mother and mother-in-law may not have an impressive legacy in worldly terms, but I know that their legacies live on in their children, grandchildren and other family members. They have taught me the importance of family, of community. They have taught me the meaning of love. Their legacy, the legacy of good mothers, is love. For that, at their feet, is Paradise.

---

1   Muslim 25:48

Home

The concept of "home" has always been a big issue in our house. The children grew up among American, German, Egyptian and Kuwaiti cultures, making them what is known as "third-culture kids" or TCKs. This special breed of people, having spent significant parts of their developmental years in a culture other than their parents' cultures, develop a sense of relationship to all of the cultures while not having full ownership in any. Our kids grew up as international travelers and cultural chameleons. They were bilingual, adaptable, and mature, with an international orientation and cross-cultural skills. But every coin has two sides, and I discovered, eventually, that my kids often felt rootless, insecure, off-balance, and unsure of where "home" was.

One of the most difficult questions TCKs are asked is, "Where are you from?" Most people automatically and confidently answer this benign question, but for a TCK, it is a conundrum. So we would joke at home about how to answer *the* question: just pick one culture that most closely resembles the one who asked; say I'm from everywhere and nowhere; say I'm from planet Earth; ask *so how much time do you have?* We would laugh and let off steam but, eventually, the conversation turned serious. We had to come to terms with the question that would trouble us our entire lives.

To put their experience in context, I told them that many prophets had trans-cultural experiences, including Abraham, Lot, Moses, Joseph, Jesus, and Muhammad. Prophets Abraham, Lot, and Muhammad left their corrupt and polytheistic homelands to establish residence where they could worship the Creator undisturbed. Moses, a true TCK, toggled between Egyptian and Israeli cultures until he finally left Egyptian civilization for life in the wilderness with the Israelites. Joseph, a son of a Levantine prophet who was sold into slavery in Egypt, undoubtedly experienced homesickness and a feeling of isolation in new surroundings. And Jesus, who fled his birthplace with his mother and Joseph to escape discovery and possible slaughter by King Herod,[2] was, essentially, homeless for some time. The experiences of these great prophets, we surmised, most certainly gave them qualities of patience, tolerance

---

2   According to Matthew 2:13-23.

and self-reliance, as well as mindsets that were inclusive, compassionate, and charitable.

We discussed Muhammad's advice to "be as a traveler" since this life is like "resting under the shade of a tree." And we agreed that Paradise is our real home – God willing – in the sense that the Garden of Eden was the original residence of Adam and Eve before they were sent to Earth, "*a place of settlement and provision for a time*" (2:36). The Quran reminded us that, "*this worldly life is only (temporary) enjoyment and, indeed, the Hereafter – that is the (permanent) settlement*" (40:39). The discussion around the prophets and the transient nature of life on Earth was helpful, but it didn't solve the need we all had to be able to identify *home* – not our dwelling place or location, but a place of identity and belonging.

I made a list of what home meant to me: the place where I belong, where I'm known, where I am welcome, where I'm comfortable to be me. It is a place where I'm not afraid to speak up, where I am accepted for who I am, where I can cry uncontrollably and laugh with all my heart. It is a place of forgiveness. Home is a familiar place where I share history and I am involved in shaping a common destiny. It's where I experience togetherness and solidarity. It is where I invest myself, feel empowered to reach a potential, and am valuable to those around me. As I realized what home meant to me, I understood what it must mean to my own children too, and hoped that they would always find home in my presence.

Since TCKs are known to find belonging in relationships rather than locations, I knew that my role as a mother was important. I had to dig deeper into my conception of home to the idea of mother, perhaps the central and most significant presence in the home. To mother is to affirm someone by letting him know it's OK to be him, as he is, that it's OK to have needs, and to take love and care from others. To mother is to care for someone enough to give him what is good for him, not just what feels good to him. It is to care about his well-being and to let him know he can depend on you no matter what. A mother is something solid to lean on and something soft to fall on. To mother is to say, in words and deeds, that you are special the way nobody else can be, and that you are loved, no matter what is or was, or will be or will not be.

Would I ever live up to this concept of mother? Would I be able to provide that sacred place called home?

My children have grown and moved away to build families of their own – another generation of TCKs in a world that thrives on inter-connectedness and cross-border movement. Like typical adult TCKs, they adapt quickly to new environments and are comfortable as outsiders. I hope they feel at home everywhere, because home is essentially a place of self-acceptance and self-worth, a place of shared values and aspirations. I hope that they are surrounded with motherly love that communicates acceptance, affirmation, and delight in the uniqueness of who they are and who they are becoming. And I hope that they extend to all they meet the prophets' gifts of compassion and inclusion. If so, I'll know that, wherever they are, they'll be home.

My Horse, My Teacher

At the age of 50 I was introduced to horses. I was at a new stage in my life in many ways and I was a bit unsure of myself as I adapted to both new and diminishing roles. I was uncertain of what I wanted to do with my life and increasingly frustrated with feelings of aimlessness. There is a saying, "When the student is ready, the teacher will appear." And so a horse appeared.

Genelli was a 23-year old mare with a generous personality. Under the direction of her owner Noelle, she had been giving rides to autistic children for ten years, the training for which made her calm in sometimes stressful situations, focused in spite of conflicting messages (between rider and leader), safe in every situation and a delight for anyone who came in contact with her. I began assisting Noelle with the rides and afterwards often had a chance to do some groundwork with Genelli. I learned basic skills in handling a horse, building trust and communicating through Pat Parelli's *Seven Games*[3] facilitated by Noelle's instruction and Genelli's patient willingness. But more importantly, Genelli allowed me to befriend her and she reassured me many times that I am an affectionate and loving person, something I was unsure of. The affection I felt towards her was reflected back with the message, "You know well how to love." She made sure I understood that before, due to a tragic accident, my time with Genelli was cut short and she was put to rest. I will always remember her as a mirror of love.

BusyBee replaced Genelli for the autistic riding program. This 23-year-old mare lacked the self-mastery and finesse that Genelli had, instead displaying a somewhat stubborn, moody disposition. Shortly after leasing her for more intensive work, I was introduced by my friend and partner Noelle to Carol Resnick's seven *Waterhole Rituals*,[4] which are based on the daily ceremonies and rituals that wild horses display in their natural environment. With them as our guide, Noelle and I planned interactions between horse and human to reinforce

---

3   Parelli, Pat. Parelli Natural Horsemanship: The Seven Games. https://www.horseillustrated.com/horse-training-parelli-seven-games. Accessed September 18, 2020.

4   Resnick, Carolyn. Introduction to the Waterhole Rituals. DVD.

appropriate behavior in BusyBee and develop the strong bond necessary for disciplined performance. The seven *Rituals* not only enhanced our understanding of each other but also gave me insight into the natural disposition of a noble animal and an opportunity to correct and refine my own.

The first ritual communicates peace by sharing territory with a horse in a non-threatening way, which is the basis for a strong bond. The horse starts to relax and will probably show some curiosity about the human in their shared space. The second ritual demonstrates respect by accommodating your horse's response to your approach to greet him. The ritual builds trust as you prove to him you have no hidden agenda; you merely wish to say hello – if he is ready. The third ritual develops a horse's awareness of you in shared territory and establishes you as a potential leader. By gently herding him away from a pile of food, you develop the horses' connection between you and both his territory and food. The fourth ritual increases the horse's focus on you. This is done by abruptly moving him away from his food whenever he stops paying attention to you. As long as he shows awareness of your position in shared territory, he is left to graze in peace. The fifth ritual enables you to lead your horse from behind, which results in him moving left, right or forward depending on your position and energy level behind him. This builds a strong bond built on trust, focus and cooperation. The sixth ritual asks for partnership as you invite your horse to walk alongside you at liberty. If the connection is strong, your horse will companion walk; however, you must maintain a leadership position and not allow your horse to start leading you! Finally, the seventh ritual culminates with your horse following your directives to move or stop at the speed you request and to come to you when asked, without a halter, bridle or rope. When this is accomplished, you and your horse are ready to work together in true harmony – this is called *the dance*. The rituals are generally sequential, but you should be ready to reinforce any of the responses by revisiting the appropriate ritual when necessary.

Helping me learn the rituals was Noelle, who is much more experienced and who has a passion for horses like no other. She would give me a summary of what to do, and then sit on the sidelines and watch. When I made a mistake she would shout "No!" and immediately correct me or jump in the paddock to show me the right way. Little by little, I began to see results with BusyBee. Within a few sessions, she was more relaxed, compliant and engaged. But each time I started a new ritual, she would get confused, worried, and frustrated – or at least that's what I sensed. I could practically hear her shouting, "What do you WANT from me?" But at some point, I realized that the voice was also my own. A voice not to Noelle, my patient instructor, but to God. Just like BusyBee, I saw myself amidst change, adopting new roles, losing old patterns, and establishing better ways to share space and communicate. I was trying hard and learning fast but, like BusyBee, I could not understand where all this was going.

It dawned on me that BusyBee was my teacher as much as I was hers. She was trying to teach me how to be, and how to be with God. I began to see how God works with us, leading us to greater awareness and willingness until we are in true harmony with Him. First by showing us His territory – this beautiful planet that is His and that He allows us to inhabit. Then by building trust in Him through His favors and by allowing us to approach Him or retreat. He also periodically establishes His authority by taking some of "our" territory – making us realize that He is entitled to our attention. With time and experience, we learn to focus on Him and, when we forget, He reminds us that we must be alert and heedful. That's exactly where I was – aware of His presence in my life and willing to follow His lead. But lately, I had been feeling imbalanced, lost, confused about which direction to go and bewildered about the whole process.

Sensing the same in BusyBee, I wanted to reassure her that everything was going to be OK. She needn't worry about her role, the future, or what tasks lie ahead. Her only job was to trust me, to focus on me and to show a willingness to be led subtly and purposefully. And that's what I must do too. Once I consistently accept God's leadership and walk every step with my focus and intention on Him, I will be living from a place of true harmony, where we are all meant to live. I don't need to know where I am going – I just need to be ready for the dance.

My Greatest Teacher

Your greatest teachers are often your toughest teachers – the ones who have strict rules, give lots of homework, and drill you until they are sure you understand the lessons they are trying to teach. Or they are the coaches who train you hard, demanding more than you thought you could handle, challenging you every day until you master the moves or continually beat your previous times. These are the people who not only believe in the value of what they teach, but even more so, they believe in your capacity for achievement and growth. They work you hard because they want you to succeed. They don't just want you to pass their test or win the race, they want to change you forever – to transform you into a confident, disciplined, and accomplished person. They want you to win. These are the people we fear, obey, respect, and eventually love. These are the people who impact our lives in untold ways, making us our best selves. We may eventually overlook the grueling work and pain of their ways, but we will never forget what we learned about ourselves and how they made us feel.

Similar in every way, Ramadan has been my greatest teacher and coach. Ramadan, the month of fasting, returns every year to remind me what I need to do to succeed, and to prove to me that I can do it. In the early years, it was about submitting my will to my Creator's will. I fasted because the Quran said, *"Those of you who see the month shall fast."* (2:185). So between dawn and sunset for 30 consecutive days, I abstained from food and drink. It was hard at first, very hard. But I did it. Year after year, I fulfilled the requirements. But Ramadan wasn't satisfied with mere compliance. There was much more to learn.

I could have cheated. Nobody could have known for sure if I was really fasting. But I didn't, and that's when fasting honed my sincerity and integrity. If I were fasting for the people, to fit in or meet social or cultural expectations, I would have cheated all those times when I missed *suhoor* and started my fast on an empty stomach. It was those days when my sincerity was tested. The Quran says, *"Fasting has been prescribed for you as it was prescribed for those before you so that you may be God-conscious"* (2:183). My mindfulness of God and sincerity to Him increased because of that great teacher, Ramadan.

The lessons spilled over into other areas of my life too. As I raised the children, pursued my Ph.D., and learned Arabic, I relied on the self-discipline, focus and motivation that Ramadan instilled in me. I knew that if I could fast for an entire month in July while those around me snacked on ice-cream and quenched their summer thirst, I could do anything – with God's help.

"It's not all about you!" said Ramadan. She taught me to think of others, those who thirst for clean water and hunger for regular meals – those who fast not by choice, but because there just isn't enough. Ramadan taught me to recognize hunger and thirst in others, which is easier when you yourself have experienced it. She taught me to respond to those in need with the compassion of one who has suffered from privation and longing, even if only for a few hours at a time. Ramadan taught me that we are responsible for one another, and that one person can make a difference in the life of another.

My teacher is persistent, still preparing lessons for me after decades under her direction. Just when I get comfortable in my routine, Ramadan comes and disrupts it, just to prove to me that in flexibility there is strength. Occasionally she challenges my complaints that I'm sick and proves to me that fasting does more good than harm, and that my health improves when I fast. She laughs when I say I'm getting old because she knows that fasting gets easier with age. Always there to challenge my attitudes, Ramadan keeps me both grounded in reality and open to the possibility of transformation.

For great teachers like Ramadan, I am immensely grateful. Grateful that I signed up, and that her tough ways and annual recurrence didn't allow me to forget a single lesson. Grateful that I could do it. Grateful that my understanding of God, self and others has expanded over time. Grateful that God Almighty extended the opportunity to me to learn under the great teacher Ramadan, just as He extends it to every one of us. Under her direction, we can embrace our potential for growth and achievement, and become more confident, disciplined, and ambitious. We can become the best versions of ourselves. For that, I thank you, Ramadan.

My Mentors

I have had many mentors throughout my life, memorable advisors who have impacted my life. Most of them, however, I have never met. They are God's prophets and messengers whose experience guide and inspire. The Quran mentions 25 prophets by name, and relates the stories of several of them in detail, such as Abraham, Solomon, Joseph, Moses, Jesus, and, of course, Muhammad. As each one has influenced me and shaped my character, it is most appropriate that I acknowledge them.

Abraham, a pillar of monotheism, taught me about faith. He is introduced in the Quran as he contemplates the stars, the moon, and the sun, exploring the fundamental nature of their existence and reality, and concluding that they are created things, not worthy of worship as his contemporaries may have believed. He furthermore asserted that, since there are created things, there must be a Creator, and that the Creator is also the sustainer of the universe, the manager of its affairs, and the only one worthy of worship in all its forms. Abraham was a philosopher-cum-theologian who, for his arguments about monotheism, was persecuted. The Quran shows how he spent his life in close communion with God and how he met the demands of that privilege. God distinguishes him with the title *al-khaleel, The Friend (of God).* Abraham's monotheistic philosophy and example of absolute faith have been a guiding light in my life.

Solomon has taught me something totally different. He was a powerful ruler of a vast kingdom. Men, jinn,[5] birds, and even the wind, served Solomon, whose kingdom was distinguished for knowledge, industry and military prowess. The verses of the Quran show that he understood the language of birds and insects, and that he was a fair judge and a skilled statesman. He was, in short, one of the most effective leaders the world has ever seen, and he taught me about good governance. Not enough to immerse myself in philosophical or spiritual pursuits, I learned from Solomon to keep one foot on the ground too, engaging

---

5   Jinn are invisible beings that live among humans but in a different dimension, and possess understanding and choice between good and evil.

with others in worldly pursuits, marveling at life and mingling with diverse others for the common good.

Joseph, son of Jacob, taught me about hope. His story is one of
rags to riches – not only in the material sense, but especially in the social sense. He experienced sibling rivalry, forced exile, slavery, temp-
tation, false accusation, and prison. His life was more interesting than
fiction with its many twists and turns, big defeats and small triumphs,
but it finally ended on the upside. All the loose ends of his story eventually resolved and he was granted all that he lost: family, status, power,
wealth, reputation, freedom. His story makes me confident that trials
have a purpose and that optimism, patience, loyalty and forgiveness
eventually pay off.

The most talked-about prophet in the Quran is Moses whose story
is told in great detail. Foster-son of the pharaoh yet biological son of the
enslaved Israelites, Moses understood the life of both the elite and the
exploited. God entrusted him with liberating the Children of Israel, not
only from the fetters of pharaoh's brutality but also from the yokes of
pagan ignorance. His task involved leading a mass exodus out of Egypt
and spending forty years in the wilderness, where a break from civilization would gradually, eventually, purge the community of tainted belief
and infuse it with pure monotheism. Moses, the great social reformer
that he was, taught me that change may begin with sudden disruption,
but actually takes decades to achieve.

Jesus is another of the great prophets and teachers of all times,
mentioned 25 times by name in the Quran. The verses confirm the virgin birth, saying that Jesus was a word ("Be!") and a spirit from God, not
unlike Adam, and confirm his miracles and his mission. Other verses
relate that he came to uphold the Mosaic law, especially the concept of
monotheism. He was tasked with the spiritual reform of the Children of
Israel, who had fallen into religious elitism and blind literalism. Having
been raised a Christian, I understood Jesus' lessons intuitively: love the
Lord your God with all your heart, all your mind, all your soul, and do
unto others as you would have them do unto you. The Quranic verses
about his life and mission removed the myths surrounding his ministry
and put his message in line with all the other prophets: *"worship Allah,
my Lord and your Lord"* (5:72).

Muhammad, descendent of Abraham through Ishmael, called the prophets mentioned above his brothers. The Quran (33:40) names Muhammad as the "seal" of the prophets and, in a beautiful analogy, he said, "The parable of myself and the prophets before me is that of a man who built a house, perfected it, and beautified it, except for the place of one brick at its cornerstone. The people walk around it and are amazed by it, and they ask, 'Why is this brick not placed?' Thus, I am the brick and I am the seal of the Prophets."[6]

I can examine Muhammad's life as thoroughly as I would a living person. His physical appearance, personal habits, spoken words and observable actions have all been described, in great detail, by those who knew him. By studying his life, I have come to realize that he was granted vast knowledge and deep wisdom like his forefathers and cousins, the great prophets we all know.

With the certain faith and singular focus of Abraham, Muhammad argued against all forms of polytheism and transformed his people from feuding pagans to loving servants of the Divine One. With the vision and wisdom of Solomon, he founded a community that then built a great empire based on knowledge, justice, and liberty. Even more than Joseph, he suffered throughout his life, and clung to decency and hope until he accomplished his mission to perfectly convey God's final message to mankind. Similar to Moses, Muhammad worked tirelessly over the span of 23 years to reform society, to replace ignorance with enlightenment, hostility with peace. In Jesus' footsteps, he demonstrated love and compassion as the overarching requirement of religious life. He was brother to all the prophets and was told, in the Quran, to "*Say, 'I am just a man like you, to whom has been revealed that your god is one God. So whoever would hope for the meeting with his Lord, let him do righteous work and not associate in the worship of his Lord anyone'*" (18:110).

These great men, and other prophets whose stories are related in the Quran, have been my mentors and guides throughout my life. They have shaped who I am and who I hope to be. They are God's prophets – my brothers in faith, my friends in God.

---

6   Bukhari 3342, Muslim 2286.

Fathers

I've had many fathers. First was my biological father, who disappeared when I was ten years old. I remember very little about him and what I do remember I'd often like to forget. He grew up in the hills of West Virginia, served in the Air Force and, by the age of 27, had six kids to feed. I don't blame him if he felt overwhelmed and unprepared for the demands of fatherhood.

My stepfather married six teenagers and their mother, and I must admit that we almost broke him. Because I had very little time with him before I left home for college, and because it was hard for both of us to connect emotionally, it took years to get to know him. But nothing showed his character more than his commitment to our family through forty years of thick and thin. Although distance separated us for most of my adult life, I was sure that if I needed him, he would be there.

I knew my father-in-law well. A global-minded professional and dynamic family man, he set high standards for himself and others. He was talkative, insightful and caring, and understood the challenges I faced as a young mother in a foreign culture. Looking back, I see how he discreetly watched over me and gently advised me while giving me the independence and privacy I was accustomed to.

Another father in my life has been my husband. Through his parenting of our children, he has healed some of the wounds and filled some of the gaps left in my own experience with fathers. His unrelenting support, protection and encouragement has enlarged my understanding of fatherhood and shaped my vision of manhood.

And then there is Muhammad, may the peace and blessings of God be upon him. This seventh-century prophet who changed world history in 23 years has made his mark on countless souls through history and around the world. He has profoundly shaped my life too and, for this reason, is a father-figure to me. For forty years now, he has been a role model and guiding light.

Every aspect of his life has been documented, deconstructed, and discussed. He was born in Mecca in 570 AD. His father died before his birth and, when he was six, his mother died in his presence after a brief illness. His grandfather took him in, but also died two years later, after which a poor uncle with several other children took him under his care. Soon Muhammad would take work as a shepherd, spending days on end in the desert. Although suffered much through childhood loss, and having no formal education, he was known among his people for his refined character and deep wisdom.

His society was a wealthy trading center and touristic destination. However, drunkenness, gambling and promiscuity were rampant. Women were objectified and exploited sexually, being regarded as property. Slavery was practiced, and the poor and helpless were denied basic rights. Gang warfare was widespread, with rivals fighting for booty, revenge, and sport. Idol worship was common, and religious customs and rituals had no basis in scripture. However, Muhammad was a firm believer in God and despised the idol worship, lawlessness, and decadence of his community.

Muhammad was not a typical teenager. Instead of spending his time partying, fighting, and gambling like his peers, he tended to the needs of the sick, poor and helpless in his community. When he was a very young man, he participated in an alliance among Meccan tribes to maintain peace in the city, suppress violence and injustice, and protect and care for the weak and destitute.

Eventually, he was able to support himself through trade. At 24, he was hired by a wealthy widow named Khadija to handle her business and earned a reputation as a conscientious and intelligent trader who was nicknamed "al-Sadiq" (the truthful one) and "al-Ameen" (the trustworthy one). Impressed by his ability, ethics and morals, Khadija proposed marriage, and he accepted. In their 25 years of marriage, they had six children, two of whom died in infancy. Muhammad spent much of his earnings caring for the needy in the community. When asked what actions are most excellent, he replied, "To gladden the heart of human beings, to feed the hungry, to help the afflicted, to lighten the sorrow of the sorrowful, and to remove the sufferings of the injured."

As he approached 40, he spent more and more time in seclusion, praying and pondering on how to reform the corruption, misery and evil of his time. At the end of a month-long retreat in a cave two miles outside of Mecca, he was visited by the archangel Gabriel and received his first revelation. Shaken and frightened, he ran home and related his extraordinary experience to his wife, who comforted him with absolute confidence and conviction. She never doubted him and was the first to believe in his mission and message.

In the 13 years that followed, Muhammad faced ridicule, persecution, assault, boycotts and assassination attempts. After fleeing Mecca, he settled in Medina where – in a mere ten years – he established a community that lived according to the Quran, protected it against treacherous hypocrites and hostile aggressors, made treaties with neighboring tribes, attracted delegations from throughout the region, and peacefully united the Arabian peninsula.

Muhammad, peace be upon him, had a very simple lifestyle, caring little for worldly comforts. He rarely ate alone, and shared what little he had with others. He was generous and never turned down anyone's request for help or material things. If asked for any of his possessions, he gave it. If he had nothing to give, he allowed the petitioner to borrow on his behalf. He was mild-mannered, never raising his voice or hand in anger or taking revenge for personal grievances. He prayed for those who persecuted him and his fellow Muslims.

He was a social activist who fed the hungry and encouraged others to do so. He carried the loads of the weak and defended the oppressed. He promoted cooperation and goodwill in the community, saying, "Do you know what is better than charity, fasting, and prayer? Keeping peace and good relations between people..." He cared for many widows and orphans, and supported women's rights, especially financial independence, self-determination, and dignity. He was an abolitionist who bought many slaves in order to set them free, and encouraged others to do so. He supported laborers and counseled people to "pay the worker his wage before his sweat dries." He said, "The best among people are those who benefit mankind" and "One who meets with others and shares their burdens is better than one who lives a life of seclusion and contemplation."

He was a leader who diplomatically mended relations with warring tribes and unified the Arabian Peninsula. He was a commander in chief who defended Medina from several attacks despite great odds. He was a head of state who dictated the Charter of Medina, one of the earliest constitutions ever written. He was so renowned for his justice that even Jews brought their suits to him to judge in accordance with their law.

To summarize Prophet Muhammad's life with these few words is a gross injustice. His outstanding character and many accomplishments pale against his success as a prophet, entrusted by the Divine Creator to relate His final message to mankind. Far from being a stern legislator or detached theologian, he was to many, and still is, a father figure. He has been a loving father to me who advised me that "People adopt the life-style of their friends, so be careful who you choose as friends."[7] He has been my teacher who instructed me to "Avoid suspicion, for suspicion is the greatest lie."[8] He has been a friend who has encouraged me with "Allah is gentle, likes gentleness, and gives for gentleness what He does not give for harshness."[9] Like a father, his influence on my life has been immeasurable. And like a daughter, I hope his legacy lives on through me. What a beautiful legacy that would be!

---

7   Al-Tirmidhi 2378

8   Al-Bukhari 6064

9   Abu Dawood 4807

Behind Every Great Man

In this age of social media, it is easy to construct a persona, which is an aspect of one's character that is presented to or perceived by others. Both influencers and ordinary people may have public personas that show them as more beautiful, affluent, happy, or virtuous than they really are. But online personas cannot mask the private lives that are witnessed by family members and close friends. Those who live with us have inside knowledge – into our true character and behavior – that outsiders do not. They see, day in and day out, who we are and what we stand for, and can be our worst critics despite their deep love and commitment to us.

In his book, *The 100: A Ranking of the Most Influential Persons in History*, Michael H. Hart cited Muhammad as the greatest influencer of all time. His Companions venerated him, as have his global followers 1450 years since. Nevertheless, like all prophets, he had many critics from within his hometown – critics who harbored arrogance, envy, and hostility. Although prior to the revelation they testified to his nobility and integrity, as soon as he called for moral reform they discredited him by calling him a liar, a madman, and a magician. They created a deceptive persona to deflect attention from their own moral failures.

But when we seek the opinion of his household, there isn't a single complaint. The person who knew him best was his wife of 25 years, Khadija. A successful businesswoman in seventh century Mecca, she was known as "Khadija the Great" and "Princess of Quraysh" because of her wealth, nobility, beauty, and philanthropy. She was a mother and twice widowed, and her hand in marriage was sought by – and unattainable to – many dignitaries of Mecca. This was the Khadija who hired the young Muhammad to accompany her caravan to Syria for trade. After proving the veracity of his popular nickname from that successful initial venture, *Al-Ameen, The Trustworthy* was contracted to lead another caravan. Upon returning with twice the expected earnings, Khadija asked her servant who accompanied Muhammad to describe how he conducted business. With a keen sense of character and impressed with the report of his impeccable reputation, she became interested in marriage and set about to propose, indirectly. Certainly the elite of Mecca were shocked that such a noble lady would seek in marriage a poor man, an orphan, one who had little of value to offer her. But Khadija, neither inexperienced in love nor desperate for marriage, knew what she wanted in life.

Muhammad and Khadija had a solid marriage and although they were busy raising six children together, they managed to serve the community through charity, hospitality, and diplomacy. They had been married for fifteen years when Muhammad came home one night pale and trembling, having experienced his first divine revelation in the cave of Hira where he had been meditating. Shocked and perplexed, he related what he experienced and his fear that he was possessed or insane. Her response was quick and firm: "By God! No! God will never disgrace you! You foster family relations, you bear the burden of the weak, you help the poor and the needy, you are generous toward your guests and you endure hardship in the path of truth." This was the moment of truth: the moment Khadija's true feelings about her husband came to the fore. She didn't doubt him, roll her eyes, or shake her head. She didn't tell him to sleep on it or take a walk – she believed in him and reassured him of his value to the community and his standing with God. She was the first to believe in his message and the staunchest supporter of his mission to spread truth and foster peace.

Many women would have complained when his – and her – reputation was smeared with accusations of fraudulence and insanity. They would have cowered when their safety and the safety of their children were jeopardized by the brutality of the opposition. They would have weakened when their very lives were threatened by a severe boycott over a span of three years that left them destitute, on the brink of starvation. But Khadija the Great, the Princess of Quraysh, never faltered, never failed to defend and support her husband and the faith they shared. Far more valuable than wealth and prestige, the values that Muhammad stood for and the man that he was imbued her with conviction, perseverance, and stamina. She proved, with words and deeds, Prophet Muhammad's genuine nobility, grace, and virtue. He was no persona. He was the Messenger of God, and she was his mirror image.

After 25 years of marriage, Khadija passed away. Muhammad grieved deeply for what was known to all as "the year of sadness." Just as she once praised him for his qualities, he declared her virtues to his companions and, through them, to every Muslim since, man or woman.

He said, "She had faith in me when people rejected me, she believed in me when people disbelieved in me. She supported me with her wealth when people prevented me…" She was a model of faith, his true counterpart.

Lady Khadija never saw the fulfillment of Muhammad's mission, nor enjoyed the triumph of a battle well fought. Her reward in this life was the companionship of her beloved Muhammad, and her reward in the next can be nothing less than union with him in Paradise.

An Enigmatic Smile

One of the companions of Prophet Muhammad said, "I haven't seen anyone smile more often than the Messenger of Allah, peace and blessings be upon him." With that, one would assume he was particularly cheerful, since smiling usually is an expression of happiness, pleasure, joy or amusement. We take that for granted. But, knowing about Prophet Muhammad's life, I find his smile a bit mysterious.

Muhammad never knew his father, since he died before he was born. His mother died when he was six – old enough to remember his loss for the rest of his life. Handed over to his paternal grandfather, he grieved his passing just two years later. He then settled with a poor uncle, working as a shepherd to earn his keep. Later, he built a family with Khadija and had six children. The two boys died as toddlers. His wife of 25 years died and then, one by one, three of his daughters died, leaving him with only the youngest, Fatima. How, after so much loss, can one continue to smile? And not just to smile, but to smile *more than anyone else*?

Muhammad was known as the Messenger of God. His duty was to convey the divine revelation to his people in Mecca and, by extension, to all mankind. He was also charged with explaining and practically demonstrating the teachings of the Quran to his followers, which might not be overly difficult in ordinary circumstances. However, doing that in the midst of ridicule, slander, assault, and attempts on his life added weight to his burden. Eventually, he fled his hometown as a refugee, finding asylum in Medina. The experience would make even the most resilient of people downcast and bitter. And yet he smiled more than any of his people.

After finding refuge in Medina, Muhammad was able to build a community based on the teachings of the Quran. It is here where he should have finally enjoyed the fruits of his labor in a society of peaceful followers. But he experienced betrayal and intrigue from the hypocrites in Medina and outright attack from the bullies of Mecca. In one conflict after another, he defended his people from brutality, robbery, and annihilation, joining the heat of battle without exception. He was always on guard, always negotiating peace, always working for stability so that he could fulfill his mission. Most men would have been plagued with worry, anxiety and fear. Yet he smiled.

His ability to hold his head high despite growing up as a poor orphan, to be happy even though he lost nearly his entire family, to carry on despite fierce opposition and brutal confrontation, and to smile throughout – to the extent that his followers said *he smiled more than anybody else* – confounds me. Where did he get his strength?

It must have been from prayer.

In spite of his heavy responsibilities, Muhammad always found time to pray. He welcomed, even waited for, the five times a day he would gather his people and lead them in prayer. He told the muezzin,[10] "O Bilal, call for prayer – give us comfort by it." When the people went home to sleep, he went home to pray, sometimes standing the whole night in devotion and supplication. He often cried in his prayers to the extent that he would wet his beard and even the mat he prostrated on.

His heart must have been broken with loneliness, trampled with brutality, stretched to bursting with fear. With that swollen, aching heart, he stood for prayer in front of his Lord, where he found a soothing presence. In that embrace, he unloaded the weight of the world from his back and cleared the sadness of tragedy from his heart until he met calm emptiness, stillness, quiet exhaustion. Then, from the Grace of God, the vacuum filled with Light! His heart swelled anew with courage and strength, peace and optimism – even joy. He overflowed with divine Love, which made him to his companions "more beautiful than the full moon." With the effects of prayer obvious in his countenance, he was able to meet everyone with an encouraging word, a charitable gesture, and a warm, genuine smile.

I can see him in my mind's eye – radiant, beautiful, smiling. May the peace and blessings of God be upon him.

---

10   A man who calls Muslims to prayer from the minaret of a mosque.

Mary

Mary, or Maryam, Mother of Jesus, is the only woman mentioned by name in the Quran. Her story is quite detailed, starting from when her mother dedicated the baby in her womb to the service of the temple (3:35). It tells how Zachariah became her sponsor (3:44), how she grew in purity (3:37), and that she guarded her chastity (19:20). It records the conversation between her and the angel who gave her the news of a child she would immaculately conceive (3:45), and how he would be a prophet of God sent to the Children of Israel (61:6). It describes her in labor (19:23), and the reaction of her astonished community when she brought her baby Jesus to them (19:27). The Quran says she was an upholder of truth (66:12) and chosen over all the women of the world (3:42).

The story of Mary is truly inspiring, but there is one phrase spoken by her that, although sounding quite ordinary, has had a deep impression on me. Chapter 3 of the Quran describes a scene where Zachariah enters her prayer chamber and finds that she has "provision." Exegeses describe the provision as out-of-season fruits, which would have been near-miraculous in Jerusalem 2000 years ago. So Zachariah asks her, "From where is this?" And she replies (in verse 37), "*It is from God. He provides for whom He wills without account.*" These wise words inspired Zachariah to ask God for a son, who would also be "out of season" due to the fact that Zachariah and his barren wife were quite old. Their son is John the Baptist, but that's another story.

I find Mary's answer to the question, "From where is this?" quite interesting. Most people probably would have said, "The neighbor sent it to me" or "A caravan has just arrived from Yemen" or "I bought it this morning from the farmers' market." Although any answer would satisfy the most curious person, it didn't satisfy her. She was so devout and so wise that she could see beyond the obvious and the circumstantial – she could see the Truth. So she answered, "It is from God." And it doesn't really matter if the provision she referred to had a mysterious origin or not. Even if Zachariah found her with her usual meal and asked, "From where is this?" I imagine she would have answered, "It is from God" because it is the truth. The Quran says, "*Whatever good has come to you, it is from God*" (4:79).

We should respond as wisely as Mary when asked about our blessings. Imagine if someone told you, I love your glasses! Where did you get them? and you said, "They are from God!" Or someone said, You look so fit! How do you do it? And you replied, "It's from God!" Or You have a lovely home. "Thanks to God! It is from Him." Or, What's for dinner? "Steak and potatoes from God." That's the outlook that Mary had: appreciative, humble, insightful. Look around and start counting your blessings – from the cup of tea beside you, to the warm blanket on your bed, to the car in the driveway. If it's good, it's from God.

And if it's not good, it's from you. The Quran says, "*Whatever good has come to you, it is from God, and whatever harm has stricken you, it is from yourself*" (4:79). Sometimes God allows something seemingly bad to happen to alert us to mistakes we are making so that we correct our actions and reform (see 30:41). Sometimes God allows bad things to happen so that we turn to Him sincerely and forsake other "gods" to whom we may have wrongly ascribed power. Sometimes we need hard times to make us more humble and receptive to spiritual guidance. Even calamaties can be blessings in disguise for those who benefit from them by turning to their Creator for solace and support. Whatever happens, we should be receptive to the good in any circumstance and count it as a blessing.

If we perceive all events in our lives as good for us – either as a source of enjoyment from God or a means of improving ourselves and growing closer to our Creator – then we can never count our blessings because they are innumerable. The Quran says that if you attempt to count the blessings of God, you could never enumerate even a *single one* (16:18), reminding us of the multifaceted goodness in a single blessing.[11] Certainly we don't deserve such continuous generosity, and we can never repay God for His care. But we can acknowledge God as the source of all good, thank Him for His blessings, and uphold the truth when we understand it. We can adopt the insight and wisdom of Mary, chosen above all the women of the world, who said about a meal, "It is from God." God's amazing response to our appreciation is this: "*If you give thanks, I will give you more*" (14:7). As Mary rightfully concluded, "He provides for whom He wills without account."

---

11   English translations of the Quran may not express the Arabic meaning correctly, perhaps due to the seeming incongruence between *blessings* and *single one*.

Singled Out from the Crowd

The teacher walked into the classroom with a big smile as I and my 20-odd classmates waited to hear our final marks. We had spent the term memorizing 20 pages of the Quran. Every Wednesday, the teacher called students one by one at random, recited a verse from within a smaller section, and evaluated our ability to continue reciting by heart from that point, with perfect pronunciation of the letters and their accompanying qualities such as elision, nasalization, and vowel elongation. Being a foreigner among native Arab students, I avoided the teacher's attention by sitting on the periphery of the classroom, out of her line of vision, hoping she would call on me last. It worked, because as she walked in, she looked to the center of the room.

"Because of your hard work and good hearts, I've decided to give each of you a full mark!" she exclaimed. The students were delighted, and blessed her for her generosity, but I shifted in my corner seat, annoyed. That's not fair, I thought. I knew I wasn't the best student in class, nor was I the worst. I wasn't happy with the extra points and would rather have gotten the 80% I figured I deserved. I felt the better students were cheated, and the poorer students were deceived. I felt invisible and, even though I had positioned myself for anonymity, suddenly I was resentful about the teacher's blanket decision. Why did it bother me when I clearly stood to benefit from the extra points?

The dissimilarity between two verses in the Quran provided a clue. The first is "*And those who were conscious of their Lord will be urged on in crowds towards Paradise until, when they reach it, they shall find its gates wide open, and its keepers will say to them, 'Peace be upon you! You have done well! So enter to stay forever!*'" (39:73) I hope to be of those led into Paradise amongst a crowd, where there will be an air of excitement and joyful anticipation, of mutual congratulations and camaraderie. But perhaps, despite the relief and thrill of the moment, I would feel just one of the masses: overlooked, insignificant and invisible in the crowd.

The second verse sets a different scene: "*and every one of them will appear before Him (God) on Resurrection Day alone*" (19:95). The prospect of being alone with God, presumably to review my earthly record of deeds, words and thoughts, was my Quran-memorizing-test anxiety multiplied by a million. The immediate reaction is dread, self-doubt, and the desire to be invisible, to get lost in the crowd, to be waved on toward my destiny without being singled out.

Which is better, I wondered: to be in the periphery and benefit from God's overarching forgiveness and generosity to the crowd? Or to sit in the examination seat in His focused attention and scrutiny as I stutter my way through? Why does it matter as long as I achieve a passing grade?

It matters to me. It matters that I am seen, faults and all. It matters that God would take the time to look at me, address me by name, listen to my voice, acknowledge my struggle, soothe my nerves, and allow me all the time I need to answer the questions on the test. It matters that I am singled out from the crowd, chosen for a brief encounter with God, whose presence I have sought for so long. Even if my mistakes are called out, it doesn't matter, because it means He noticed me. It means I wasn't invisible. It means I mattered, even just a little, to Him.

I pray that the day I meet God will be my best day ever, and that my meeting alone with Him, after a lifetime of focus and practice, will get me the passing mark. And I would not foolishly object if He, in His overarching generosity, said, "Full mark!" despite my mistakes. Afterwards, it would be nice to join my colleagues from Life on Earth for a graduation party, and to walk in crowds toward the open doors of Paradise. In that moment, I will know how special it is to be singled out, among the crowd.

2

REFLECTION

2

Reflection

If life is a journey, we are all travelers. Every step takes us closer to our destination, which is none other than what we intentionally and actively seek. Becoming aware of our agency in shaping our destiny is often a gradual process. We gradually gain experience and gather insights that can lead us toward our best selves. We learn to ask the right questions, to follow signs and intuition, to trust that God is helping us on our way, and that every difficulty shall pass.

Two things have helped me on my journey to find God – life itself and His guidebook, the Quran. Each is an abundant source of wisdom, waiting to be explored, examined, and understood. This section dissects basic concepts that have been essential for my understanding of God, such as freedom, trust, faith, and choice, as well as the paradigms that shape my experience with Him, such as respect, patience, and faith. I have relied heavily on the Quran to inspire and guide me in choosing a destination and drawing a map for my journey forward.

What truths have you realized, through reflection or actual experience, that have clarified your sense of purpose and your direction in life?

Signs

I was driving home one day when I spotted this sign on the road: "Camera ahead – 80." I thought, how nice of the traffic department to warn us that a camera is ahead and remind us that the speed limit is 80 km/hr. I drove ahead and looked for the camera. Sure enough, about 100 meters from the sign was the camera, barely visible behind a tree branch. That sign is one of the many that are placed along the road – they warn us of danger, give us directions or information, prohibit certain actions, and even relate good news such as "sale!" or "opening soon." To all those who invest in signs to help us on our way – thank you.

Not only on the roads are there signs. God said He placed them throughout the universe and within our own selves. But what do they say and where do they lead? For those who think, ponder, and reflect, the signs tell them a lot about the Creator of our world and relate certain facts of our existence. Unfortunately, we do not always pay attention to the natural phenomena around us or analyze their meanings. So our Creator did us a great favor by spelling out His signs in a more obvious way. One by one, over 6,000 signs are catalogued in human language in what is known as the Quran. The "signs" share information, give directions, demarcate boundaries, prohibit dangerous actions, relate good news and give very clear warnings. Here is a sample of God's signs from the Quran:

Information: *God (Himself) bears witness that there is no god but Him, as do the angels and those with knowledge – He is the One upholding justice. There is no god but Him, the Almighty, Most Wise.* (3:18)

Directions: *...And establish regular prayer for My remembrance.* (20:14)

Prohibitions: *...Indeed, intoxicants and gambling... are but defilement from the works of Satan, so shun them so that you may be successful.* (5:90)

Good news: *Verily, the dwellers of Paradise that Day, will be busy in joyful things. They and their spouses will be in pleasant shade, reclining on thrones. They will have therein fruits (of all kinds), and all that they will ask for. "Peace" shall be the word from a Merciful Lord.* (36:55-58)

Investment opportunities! *Who is he that will lend to God a goodly loan so that He may multiply it for him many times over?* (2:235) *Indeed, the charitable men and the charitable women who have loaned God a goodly loan shall have it multiplied for them by their Lord. So for them, there is a gracious reward awaiting in the Hereafter.* (57: 18)

Advice: *Do not turn your cheek to people in contempt, and do not walk upon the Earth proudly exultant. Indeed, God loves no one who is smug, boastful.* (31:18)

Warnings: *Indeed, God will not forgive associating any god with Him. But He forgives anything less than this for whomever He so wills. Thus, whoever associates gods with God has truly strayed far astray!* (4:116) *Truly Hell is waiting – a destination for the transgressors.* (78: 21-22).

Corrections: *Righteousness in the sight of God is not the mere turning of your faces toward the East or the West. Rather, true righteousness dwells in one who believes in God and the Last Day, and in the angels, and the Book, and in the prophets; it dwells in one who, despite his love for it, gives of his wealth in charity to close relatives and orphans, and to the indigent and the wayfarer, and to beggars and for the emancipation of slaves; it dwells in one who establishes the Prayer and gives charity, and those who fulfill their covenant when they make a covenant, as well as in those who are patient during periods of affliction and harm and times of conflict. These are the ones who have been truehearted, and it is such as these who are the God-fearing.* (2:177)

The signs are presented in various ways and repeated often to make sure the reader understands them and the correlations between them. Some of the signs mention the signs themselves:

"(Here) indeed are signs for a people that are wise" (2:164). *"Thus does God make clear His signs to you, in order that you may be guided"* (3:103). *"We will show them Our Signs in the universe, and in their own selves, until it becomes manifest to them that this [Qur'an] is the Truth"* (41:53).

Whether traffic signs or verses of guidance, without signs around us, we would be perpetually lost. To those who post signs to help us on the road, and to our Creator who guides us on our path through life – thank You!

Kindness

I'll never forget that kiss – an unexpected display of affection from BusyBee. I had leased her to improve my equestrian skills and with the hope of training her for a therapy program for autistic children. But she had a bad reputation. Her owner had given up on her, saying she was moody and not fit for riding. She became agitated when mounted, often refused commands, and was generally unpredictable. I was told that her previous owners were rough with her and punished her harshly when she didn't perform well. But she was the only horse available, so I took her under my care.

I could feel her dissatisfaction and mistrust from the beginning. Just walking her around the equestrian grounds was a challenge. Not wanting to follow my lead, she decided she would dominate the walks and lead *me* around. She would yank at the rope, quicken her pace ahead of me, and veer off the path I set. Testing my limits, she would often balk, occasionally rear and once dealt me a swift kick to my leg during a walk. It was hard to maintain my composure, to meet her unpredictable moods with firm yet calm resolve, and to consistently treat her with respect and loving care – characteristics I had hoped to instill in her so that she could be a reliable therapy horse.

Work continued week after week and, like her owner, I almost gave up. But after each session, no matter how frustrating it was, I would stroke her affectionately, sympathizing with her early trauma and acknowledging her dignity and worthiness for love. Then, as I stroked her flank one day, she suddenly turned to me and kissed me! From that day, she transformed into a willing trainee and became everything I had hoped she could be. As a therapy horse, she was composed, compliant, reliable and, most importantly, safe for the autistic riders that fidgeted on her back, day after day.

My experience with a horse provided insight into people who behave with suspicion, insult or hostility. I believe that people hurt others because they themselves are hurting. I don't need to know the details of their lives to sense their underlying pain or shortage of love. If I can look beyond their hurtful and aggressive words and deeds and react instead to a troubled soul or a broken heart, I can more easily choose compassion and kindness. When I am tempted to react to belligerent people with similar belligerence, I hear the Quranic advice, "*The good deed and the evil deed are not alike. Repel (evil) by that which is better, and then the one between you and him is enmity will become as though he was a devoted friend*" (41:34). Overriding my gut reaction to retaliate, and deliberately choosing a wholesome and positive response, takes self-control, confidence and patience. A measured response is not always easy.

The Quran supplements its advice to reply to evil with good with a qualifier: "*But none attains to this except those who are patient, steadfast...*" (41:35). The verse reminds me that I should not expect an immediate positive response to a single act of kindness. I will need to forgive and be kind repeatedly and consistently to prove to the offender that I value him. Having dignity, I must dignify others, even when they are vulgar. And just as I wish to be treated with kindness, I should be kind to others, even if they make themselves seem unworthy of it. How could I hope for forgiveness if I myself cannot forgive?

Eventually, love pays off. BusyBee's kiss was a sign that kindness had mended her heart. She told me she was ready to love in return and since then she has touched autistic children in ways I cannot fully understand. But seeing them riding BusyBee, smiling brightly, I realized that she had become the therapy horse of my dreams, with more to give than I ever imagined. Most of all, BusyBee taught me that patient kindness will eventually triumph and then carry forward in untold ways.

Happiness

A question that nags me from time to time is, "What is the goal of my life?" The pursuit of happiness seems to be a universal aspiration, yet I'm not sure it's mine. I have appetites that demand satisfaction, ambition that propels me to achieve, and a psyche that seeks love, belonging and respect. In short, I want to be happy both physically and emotionally, which requires a degree of material and social success. I don't deny that I want to be happy, and yet I would feel selfish to say that the *goal* of my life is to be happy. So let's just say that happiness is one of the driving factors in my life.

What if God told us, "I have created you to be happy"? Would life then have more meaning as we pursue whatever pleased our bodies, souls, and egos? Where would that lead us? What if what made me happy would eventually lead to my ruin? What if what made me happy made someone else miserable? What if everyone's feeling of entitlement to happiness led people to hostility, crime, and war? If our sole aim in life was happiness, I think we would be miserable.

Although I believe God does want us to be happy, He declared in the Quran that He created us so that we may devote ourselves to Him – to worship Him (51:56) – but not for His satisfaction, as He is not in need of our worship. Worshipping God, it seems, might be the way to achieve well-being and ultimate happiness. **Which makes me wonder, what does worship have to do with happiness?**

Worship to some may seem like a distinctly un-enjoyable activity, one that involves self-denial or a disciplined rejection of pleasurable experiences. However, by creating us to worship Him, God didn't mean we should spend our lives in secluded prayer. There is overwhelming evidence in the Quran that He expects us to lead lives with rich physical and emotional experiences, satisfying activities in all spheres of life and fulfilling relationships with others. Even though God created us to worship Him, He makes it clear that our environment and our abilities are to be enjoyed with gratitude and within His limits.

Like a loving parent who wants the best for his child, God wants the best for us. Like a loving parent who works hard to provide a comfortable life for his child, God created the whole Earth for our use. And like a loving parent who tells her child to "eat your vegetables," "brush your teeth," and "do your homework," God has suggestions and advice that will make us happy eventually. They are suggestions because God doesn't compel anyone to follow them. But like the loving child who follows his parents' rules with faith and trust, the believer takes God's suggestions very seriously. To one who believes in God's authority, a mere suggestion is an order, but to one who values his own opinion foremost, even a clear order is viewed as a mere suggestion.

Our parents' rules of how to live right are ingrained in us, and we see the benefits of following such advice. Likewise, God's rules are there for our benefit, and provide a framework for personal, material, emotional and social happiness. By obeying God's rules, we acknowledge His knowledge of what will lead us to ultimate happiness. Worship, it seems, is to follow God's suggestions while believing in His authority, with happiness being the expected and eventual outcome.

My instruction manual for achieving personal and social happiness – both short-term and long-term – is the Quran. It is there that I find the connection between worship and happiness, and the answer to that nagging question, "What is the goal of my life?"

Faith

If an alien from space landed in the parking lot of a hospital, and from there learned about life on Earth, he would be shocked. At the Emergency Entrance, he might see people being strapped down, taken unwillingly into the hospital. Inside, he would witness doctors cutting people open, removing organs, poking needles, drawing blood, injecting poisons, performing many painful procedures, and making people suffer, sometimes until they die. He would witness pain, fear, and grief in the hospital walls and, out of ignorance, believe that doctors are cruel and heartless. That understanding, however, is due to the observer's ignorance of the *purpose* of medicine and the *methods* that are used to restore physical health.

Likewise, someone with little or no faith in the *purpose* of life and the *methods* used to achieve those purposes will not understand the care and compassion that is behind the often difficult circumstances of our lives, circumstances that are perhaps tailored to our specific experience, traits and needs in order to help us reach our best selves. The purpose of our earthly life is very clearly stated in the Quran and gives us a framework for our lives. "*[He] created death and life to test you [as to] which of you is best in deed...*" (67:2). The methodology is also clear: "*And We will certainly test you with something of fear and hunger and a loss of wealth and lives and fruits...*" (2:155-156) "*...and We test you with evil and with good as trial...*" (21:35).

With these watchwords in mind, I should expect both good times and hard times, and shouldn't get disheartened when I experience the hard times. Perhaps I can make the journey easier by learning about God's vision for me – asking myself, what does He want from me? How does He want me to live? Maybe I can help myself by doing things right, and by taking more responsibility for my own personal health and growth, avoiding what I can of difficult and painful situations.

People say life would be easier if there was an instruction manual. Our Creator did not overlook such a necessity. He sent us a textbook for life – the Quran – as well as a teacher to explain and exemplify it. I have faith that my Creator knows what is good for me and what will make me strong. He may see a potential champion in me but, in coaching me to my greatest strength, He requires training, sacrifice and endurance,

which often translates as hard work, soreness and pain. Most certainly, my compassionate Lord wants my soul to be healthy, and He gives
me the nourishment I require, as well as the medicines and treatment
I occasionally need to regain optimal health. When life is hard, I go to
my Lord as I would go to my doctor – trusting his expertise, expecting
prescriptions and proscriptions based on his diagnosis, and willing to
do what is necessary to become my best self.

If God Wills

I bumped into a friend last week. She had a massive bruise on her forehead. What happened? I asked. "I was hit by a heavy casserole dish!" My confusion was apparent, so she explained. The previous week had been quite hectic, making her as sleep deprived as a new mother. She was excited at the prospect of sleeping early one night and sleeping in late the next day, which was a holiday. She announced her intention to nobody in particular, determined that nothing would stop her from a good night's sleep. And on her way to bed, she stopped in the kitchen and, on the spur of the moment, decided to put away the casserole dish from last night's dinner. As she lifted it to place it on a high kitchen shelf, the lid atop it slid off and hit her square on the forehead. Afraid that she might have suffered a concussion, she forced herself awake for hours, and her will to sleep was overridden by the lid of a casserole dish.

That story sounds familiar, I thought to myself. I had been reading a short chapter of the Quran, al-Qalam, which tells the story of the owners of an orchard who resolved to harvest their crop at dawn the next day in order to avoid the poor folk of their community and deprive them of expected charitable portions. But when they arrived at the place of the orchard, they saw a field that had been stricken by fire during the night. Initially thinking they were lost, they realized that their orchard was utterly consumed and said, "*Alas, we are the deprived ones.*" A central verse comprised of two words in the midst of the story – following their vow to harvest their crop – means, "*they made no reservation.*" The rhythm of the section is such that this truncated phrase in the middle is quite noticeable and makes the reader pause for a moment. Obviously, it is one of the morals of the story.

What do a bump on the head and a burnt orchard have in common?

They remind us that, no matter how determined we are to do something, how resolved we are in our decision, how perfect our plan, and how complete our preparations, we must always acknowledge that there is Knowledge deeper, a Plan better, and a Will stronger than ours. Our Creator knows best and does what He wills, regardless of our own willfulness. Never should we assume that we know best or have absolute control. Never should we assume an unconditional will.

This doesn't mean that we shouldn't have a plan or do everything possible to achieve our goals, but rather that we have to subordinate our will to that of our Lord, which can be done by simply adding, "If God wills" to our plans. Then, when our plans go wrong, we can accept that there is wisdom in the outcome, and when our plans are realized, we can gratefully acknowledge God's support.

Every now and then we might forget. But if we're paying attention, something as simple as a casserole dish will remind us of our conditional will.

Optimism

I love stories with happy endings. In fact, I expect happy endings. It's part of my American culture – the "happily ever after" promise ingrained in me through fairy tales and childhood dreams. Perhaps believing in happy endings is in our nature – by default, we incline towards virtue, recognize good and expect positive resolutions. Or perhaps we are disillusioned and endings are random and unpredictable, as often sad as they are happy. I hope not. But there are times in life when a happy ending seems elusive, even impossible. So what should we realistically expect?

When I have questions or doubts, I turn to God for answers. I recall the stories in the Quran – stories of separation, heartache and sacrifice – and trace their events until the end. The "best of stories" in the Quran is that of Joseph (chapter 12). A recurring theme of his life is separation. His siblings, jealous of their father's extraordinary love for Joseph, separate him from his family by throwing him into a well, where he is recovered and sold into slavery. After reaching maturity in the home of the Minister (Aziz) in Egypt and becoming the object of the Minister's wife's infatuation, he is again separated, through false accusation, from his new family and thrown in prison for several years. When he interprets a dream for the king, he is released from prison and made vizier[12] of Egypt, eventually meeting his brothers, who come to barter their goods for grain. The story ends happily with the scene of a joyful reunion with all of Joseph's family in Egypt.

The story of Moses' mother also grabs my attention. Being a mother myself, I can feel her panic and despair when she casts her infant into the river in order to save him from the Pharaoh's slaughter. Although Moses was rescued and adopted by the Pharaoh's wife, his mother's instinct made her heart "empty [of all else]" to the point that she almost disclosed Moses' identity had not God strengthened her resolve. Then, through a miraculous turn of events, Moses was *returned to his mother so that she might be content and not grieve, and so that she would know that the promise of Allah is true. But most people do not know*" (28:13). The beauty of this story, to me, is that although Moses

---

12   A high official, likely deputy to the king.

was safe and cared for in Pharaoh's palace, God returned him to his true mother to tenderly soothe her broken heart and increase her faith. Another happy ending.

Finally, the story of Abraham reinforces my belief in ultimate happiness. He saw in a dream that he would sacrifice his only son, Ishmael. Such sacrifice is impossible under any circumstances, and the love Abraham must have had for the boy made it infinitely more difficult. This boy was his long-awaited son, to whom Abraham was most certainly a devoted and loving father. When Ishmael finally reached the age when he could interact with his father as a young man, Abraham had the dream, which he may have interpreted as a test of fidelity – to prove to God that he loved Him more than his most beloved son, more than his own happiness, more than life itself. So as he lay his son down for the sacrifice, the Lord called him, *"O Abraham! You have fulfilled the vision!"* (37:105). Having proven his devotion to God beyond any shadow of a doubt, a ram appeared, and it was sacrificed instead of Ishmael.

During the Covid-19-induced lockdown, I saw tragedy all around me. Some lost their loved ones, others their livelihood, and many struggled with the uncertainty of when, if ever, things would get back to normal. Tragedy is intertwined in the human experience and necessary, I believe, to imbue value in the precious moments when things are going right. How can we understand love unless we've lost it? How can we appreciate happiness if we've never been sad? Love and happiness can be fully appreciated only in the context of *contrast* – in this sense, tragedy may be just as valuable as happiness. Sorrow and joy may be twin souls in the sense that one cannot be experienced without the other.

An Irish proverb states that "Everything will be alright in the end. If it's not alright, it's not the end." By examining Quranic stories to their very end, I tend to agree. Even though some stories end, temporarily, in loss or death for God-conscious, upright protagonists,[13] the verses that follow their stories promise a happy-ever-after of another kind. As eloquently expressed in the Quran, "[in Paradise] you will have all that your souls desire, and there you will have all that you ask for." (41:31) "... gardens of perpetual residence ...abiding therein forever... (98:8).

---

13   See, for example, the story of Pharaoh's magicians in the Quran, 20:70-76.

Whether happiness is achieved sooner or later, God's promise is far from fairy tales and wishful thinking. Since His promise is necessarily true, I will always believe in happily ever after.

Midway

 Imagine a bridge between two mountain tops. Not an ordinary bridge, but one made of ropes and planks, one that swings precariously in the wind, one whose gaps are as wide as its footing. And you have started walking across the bridge – perhaps because it was the only path in front of you, or perhaps it was the path to where you had planned to go. Halfway across, you get scared. You realize the risks. You doubt your strength to go forward. You freeze midway between the two mountaintops and weigh your options, a vacuum all around you. You decide to go back, to retrace your steps and forget about reaching the other side. But when you turn around to backtrack to safety, you see that the planks on the bridge have blown away from the ropes, and that what is left of the bridge is enveloped in misty clouds, making a return impossible. And so there you stand. Behind you a fading memory, below you an abyss, before you a painful trek through fear, doubt, and exertion to a place whose promise is illusive. And you have no choice but to go forward, one step at a time, to the unknown.

 I've been there. Perhaps you have too. It's a scary, lonely place to be.

 Nothing will get you to the other side except a little faith. It is faith that led me forward – faith that God could see me, faith that He knew my predicament, and faith that if He allowed me to stand in that midway place, that it was where I was supposed to be.

 The story of Moses held my attention through my struggle to the other side. After hearing God's voice near the burning bush and discussing the task to address the Pharaoh, Moses was told: *And we had already conferred favor upon you another time when We inspired to your mother what We inspired, saying, "Cast him into the chest and cast it into the river, and the river will throw it onto the bank; there will take him an enemy to Me and an enemy to him." And I bestowed upon you love from Me that you would be brought up under My eye [and care]. [And We favored you] when your sister went and said, "Shall I direct you to someone who will be responsible for him?" So We restored you to your mother that she might be content and not grieve. And you killed someone, but We saved you from retaliation and tried you with a [severe] trial. And you remained some years among the people of Madyan. Then you came [here] at the decreed time, O Moses (20:37-40).*

The favors to Moses were many, and God recounts some of them: being saved from Pharaoh's slaughter by being cast into a river – only to be adopted by the Pharaoh himself – and being raised in Pharaoh's household, yet having access to his mother and his people…. he was torn between two peoples, two cultures, two classes, two families. There were other favors: being spared reprisal for an unintended crime, finding refuge among yet another people in a different land – Madyan. And finally, the words that resounded in my soul:

Then you came here at the decreed time, O Moses.

An ordinary day wandering in the desert of Sinai and all the weird and unusual events that led him to that fateful conversation with God Himself were highlighted for Moses as God's *decree, blessing,* and selective *care.*

With a little introspection, I retraced the steps that led me to the middle of the bridge where I could no longer see past or future, where I almost gave up if not for the faith that called me forward. I gradually began to see the Divine Care in my life, and when I opened my heart to His continual presence, I could feel great love and direction from none less than God Almighty. I could feel Moses' wonder at how God had prepared him, acknowledged his struggles and anticipated his arrival, and his realization of God's caring, nurturing, protective guidance. All the events of Moses' life prepared him for that moment with God and the great task assigned to him. With faith he honored God's command. With faith he walked forward, one step at a time. And with faith, I was able to cross the bridge that finally led me to solid ground and peace of mind.

Freedom

Freedom is such a powerful word. But what does it imply? Freedom *from* something or freedom *to do* something?   It could mean different things to different people, but the dictionary defines it as the power or right to act, speak, or think as we want without hindrance or restraint.   So it means both freedom *from* hindrance and freedom to think, speak, and act.

The fact is that everyone is free – that's the way God made us. We are free to think as we like. We are free to speak as we like. And we are free to act – within the limits of our human ability – as we like. It's the consequences of saying and doing what we want that worry us. We think that if we face unpleasant *consequences* for saying or doing what we like, we are not free. So what people really want when they long for freedom is freedom from *consequences*.

Freedom to say and do everything we want without facing any unpleasant consequences is unrealistic because it disregards others' rights. For example, because of the Covid 19 pandemic, we are all now keenly aware of the effect that one person's illness can have on others, and we appreciate the self-imposed quarantine of those who think they may be contagious.   We are faced with the reality that our actions bear consequences, and knowing that deflates our sense of freedom. Nevertheless, having freedom and avoiding unpleasant consequences is possible. We just have to *want* pleasant consequences enough to freely *choose* the things that make them possible! Actually, most of us practice this in our daily lives. For example, we want to have good health and to avoid the possibility of certain diseases, so we freely adopt hygiene and healthy eating habits to achieve that. We are all free to eat junk food and smoke cigarettes, but we choose not to do it because we are planning ahead for more comfortable outcomes.

God helps us to make good and wholesome choices, whether they are physical, social or spiritual. For example, when we do something healthy, we feel good – like taking a brisk walk in the morning. When we do a good deed for another person, we feel happy even though we may have exerted effort or given up something we value. Even when we do something personal and unnoticed by others – such as a prayer in the depths of the night – we feel good. God has helped us by hardwiring us to feel happy when we freely make good choices.

Many times we make choices that give us the solution we need or gratification we crave, yet eventually lead to complications and even misery. Whether about personal habits, finances or relationships, God has taken some of the guesswork out of major decisions by giving us advice. For example, if we look in the Quran, we find several prescriptions – for example, for sobriety, modesty and forbearance – as well as prohibitions – from interest, gambling, and promiscuity, to name a few. God promises that "*Whenever guidance from Me comes to you – then for those who follow My guidance, they shall not fear nor shall they grieve*" (3:38). We try our best to follow God's advice because we know that it will bring us happiness – if not immediately, then eventually.

This promise encourages us to be proactive by taking positive measures to avoid the occurrence of a future problem. For example, God forbids both promiscuity and intoxicants, which may initially appear to be an infringement of our freedom. Yet when we think about it, we realize how it saves us from the devastating consequences of such "freedom," such as STDs, unwanted pregnancies, abortions, alcoholism, drunk driving, drug addictions, and drug-related crimes, in addition to the psychological, social and financial toll of such bad habits. Proactivity requires forethought and restraint, but it can save us from cascading and irreversible hardship.

But sometimes, even though we make all the right choices, we face unpleasant, unhappy situations. For example, we can get a disease even though we eat well, exercise, and don't smoke. Is that fair? How can we feel free when something like that happens? Actually, we are still free — free to choose our response. We can freely choose not to be overwhelmed by emotional pain such as anger or despair. We can freely choose patience and trust in God, because we know that He is the one in charge of this universe, that He does things for our benefit, and that He does not make mistakes. We can look at God's promise for the *future* also as instructions for the *present*: "*...those who follow My guidance, they shall not fear nor shall they grieve*" (3:38). So not only does a free person make good choices that help him avoid unpleasant consequences, he also chooses confidence and contentment, even when life is difficult.

Some people don't understand that. When they see someone happily choosing a lifestyle that, from their perspective, is restrictive or uncomfortable, they think that he is ignorant, oppressed or forced to act that way. They forget that every person is free. As a Muslim, I am answerable, first and foremost, to God, which frees me from many things: from concern over the judgment of others, from bad choices that end in misery, and from distress over things beyond my control.

Everybody wants the freedom to seek pleasure and happiness without facing unpleasant consequences, and I do too. But my *approach* to achieving that is different; I carefully and deliberately exercise my freedom by choosing good thoughts and doing good deeds, focusing on God as my judge. This approach is a long term plan whose gradual implementation is satisfying and rewarding. Each small achievement is gratifying in itself and is a step on the path toward ultimate happiness. It is the path that bestows true freedom, cultivates deep contentment, and surprises me with an exhilarating sense of happiness.

A Good Life

At the age of 94, after a brief illness, my father-in-law Yousef passed away. Gripped with grief, his children informed family and friends, arranged the funeral and sent an obituary to the newspapers. Condolences started trickling in – phone calls and messages that served as a virtual reception in Covid times. The following days stunned us. Hundreds of people from around the world contacted his children and grandchildren to express their sympathies and share how he impacted their lives. As the tributes poured in, we transitioned from mourning death to celebrating life. Yousef's death showed us what it means to live a good life.

His life was not one of indulgence. He grew up during the Great Depression, which not only conditioned him to live modestly, but also taught him to respond to those in need. Although his unimpressive salary from various posts in public education could have been enough to build a small retirement fund, he was benefactor to both immediate and distant family members who turned to him in hard times or whom he himself sought when he had more than he needed. For twelve years after his retirement at the age of 82, he continued to help siblings, cousins, in-laws and distant relatives from his pension, and bequeathed a significant portion of his estate to their welfare.

Loyalty was one of his defining characteristics. He married his childhood sweetheart and was a loving and faithful husband for nearly 70 years. To his wife he was respectful and kind, generous and warm. In their old age they were inseparable, together facing one limitation after another with cheerfulness and affection. To his children he was supportive and encouraging, involved and inspiring. They share stories of how he taught them self-reliance, respect for others, good manners and integrity. His son summed it up: "He was a man, in its true sense, which means carrying responsibility, working hard for the right, persevering to reach results, being true to your word, valuing family, and respecting and loving your wife."

Although he always made time for family – and his idea of family was indeed wide – his life's passion was education. He was, at heart, a teacher, and his goal was to transform lives through education. Starting his career as an Arabic teacher in a public school, and eventually retiring as director of Kuwait's many vocational education colleges, he was intimately familiar with every stage of education and its promises and challenges. But his administrative roles did not distance him from the individual beneficiaries of his relentless struggle to educate a nation, and many people called to bear witness to the great impact he had on their lives. High-school dropouts turned professors, teenage delinquents turned devout Muslims, and countless others were fundamentally changed by his vision, wisdom and impassioned care. His ways were sometimes subtle – he once gifted me with a Quran and wrote a dedication inside the cover. Although he knew I could read neither the Arabic scripture nor the words he lovingly inked in, his gesture told me that he had faith that someday I would, and he was right.

Yousef's family was awed by the comments of those who should have long forgotten him, yet could not. We were comforted by people from all walks of life who took the time to share their memories and offer condolences. The recognition of his achievements, both big and small, attested to the life he led – the good life – which has reaped goodness in this life and, undoubtedly, will have its reward in the next.

Although not everyone can be a world-class educator, we can all live a good life. For example, Yousef's wife worked just as hard as he did, her sacrifices were as great or greater, and her patience was unmatched. Although few people knew her, God knows her, and that's what matters. God says that *"Whoever does good, whether male or female, while he is a believer – We will surely cause him to live a righteous life..."* (16:97). The good life is not to be measured by man-made criteria such as wealth, beauty, good times or "likes." The good life is more than the thrills this world can offer. It sometimes means resisting impulsive desires and whims, and seeking God's approval by serving Him and His creation. God asks, *"Do those who commit ill-deeds suppose that We shall make them live as those who believe and do good works, so their lives and death are the same? Bad is their judgment!"* (45:21).

Yousef's life was characterized by reliance on God, loving relationships, faith in human potential, meaningful work, modesty, and integrity. His was a life worth celebrating. His was a good life.

R-E-S-P-E-C-T

Do you remember a song performed by Aretha Franklin entitled "Respect"? It begins with "What you want... baby, I got. What you need, you know I've got it. All I'm askin' is for a little respect...R-E-S-P-E-C-T. Find out what it means to me!" Generally interpreted as being about respect between genders and especially for women, this powerful song that asks for a little respect has become a classic.

Respect as a concept is highly valued in today's world. It is comprised of both an *attitude* of appreciation toward another as well as specific *conduct* that honors the other. Respect is politically correct, and anyone would agree that upright citizens respect each other. Because some people need reminders and a little help, there is a group to advocate respect for just about every sector of society there is. We are told to respect the opposite sex, the unborn child, the homosexual, the handicapped, the mentally ill. We are reminded that everyone has rights, including children, the dying, people of every race and creed, and even animals. We are expected to respect the environment, the dead, and the right of others to eat and shop in a smoke-free environment. Respect is so important, that we have learned to respect the mere *concept* of respect.

We would be exemplary citizens if we respected all the things we are expected to respect. And we would know what to do because we know the universal adage "do unto others as you would have them do unto you." But how would we express the ultimate respect – respect for God? Unfortunately, applying the "do unto others" rule doesn't apply to our relationship with God because He is unlike us – He is God.

It is my guess that some of us who practice respect for all others have overlooked God, perhaps because He doesn't file lawsuits or publicize others' poor treatment of Him in the media. If there was a group that promoted and protected the rights of God for our respect, what would they teach us? First, they would have to expose the reality of how we treat God in order to bring attention to the severity of the problem. They would show us that we overlook, trivialize, marginalize, ignore and even deny the very existence of God. They would probably bring to light some of God's positive qualities so that we can appreciate Him more: His omniscience, omnipotence, generosity, forbearance and forgiveness. They would show proof of His goodness, such as the presence of so much beauty on Earth, how He provides water and grows food for eight billion people and countless animals, and how He protects the inhabitants of this fragile planet in innumerable ways. And they would expose the fact that in spite of all that, many people mistrust Him, bad-mouth Him, and offend Him regularly, showing gross disrespect.

Perhaps after being educated by the advocates-for-God group, we would be more inclined to respect Him. But if we *really* want to respect God we should try to know *how* He wants to be respected – which attitudes and conduct does he expect from us? We can find many clues in the Quran.

Those who respect God show gratitude: *"God brought you out of your mothers' wombs knowing nothing at all, and gave you hearing, sight and hearts so that perhaps you would show thanks"* (16:78). *"Eat of the good things We have provided for you and give thanks to God..."* (2:172). *"Why should God punish you if you are thankful and believe?..."* (4:147).

Those who respect God remember Him: *"Mankind! Remember God's blessing to you. Is there any creator other than God providing for you from heaven and Earth?..."* (35:3). *"(Believers are those) who remember God, standing, sitting, and lying on their sides, and reflect on the creation of the heavens and the Earth..."* (3:191).

Those who respect God pray to Him: *"Seek help in patience and prayer. But that is a very hard thing, except for the humble."* (2:45) *"Believers are those who safeguard their prayers"* (23:9).

Those who respect God worship none but Him: *"Worship God and do not associate anything with Him..."* (4:36). *"We sent no messenger before you without revealing to him: 'There is no god but Me, so worship Me'"* (21:25).

Why is it so easy for some people to respect every person, regardless of his worthiness of respect, yet so hard to respect their Creator who asks for so little in return for so much? Respect isn't something we offer to God, but rather something that belongs to Him already. So will we give Him what is rightfully His? Or will we overlook, trivialize, marginalize, ignore, and deny Him? What is the respect we owe God? He told us: *"I am Allah. There is no god but Me, so worship Me and perform prayer to remember Me"* (20:14). All He's askin' is for is a little respect … R-E-S-P-E-C-T.

Trust

All my life I've tried to be independent – independent in the sense of relying on myself as much as possible to get things done. As an American, I have been socialized to value independence as a positive aspect of a strong character. In addition, my early experiences through the filter of childhood and adolescence conditioned me to depend on myself foremost, thereby avoiding the painful possibility that in a moment of need I would not find someone I could trust, someone dependable.

As a Muslim, however, I am taught to depend on God. There are many verses in the Quran that urge me to trust and depend on God, such as, *"If God helps you, no one can defeat you. If He forsakes you, who can help you besides Him? So upon God should the believers rely"* (3:160). *"And (He will) provide for him from where he has never conceived. Whoever relies on God – He will suffice him...."* (65:3).

I have read the verses many times and, on an intellectual level, I understand them, agree with them, and try to apply them. I have tried to trust God and depend on Him. And generally, I feel I do. But every now and then I find myself in a corner, or in grave need, and the verses come to mind. I hear a gentle message: *"Trust* Me." And I realize then that I haven't really been trusting God at all, nor have I been depending on Him. At least not enough.

Can we trust someone spontaneously? Or is it something that develops over time? How do we develop trust in someone? How long should it take?

In my experience, it takes a long time to trust someone and depend on him – it may take years. It seems to me that there are different variables in the formula of trust, and the variables should be tested under different conditions to determine their strength or value. One of the variables is knowledge, and a second one is wisdom. For example, I wonder if the doctor I confide in with my health concerns has enough knowledge to diagnose the problem and enough wisdom to prescribe the right treatment for me. Another variable is ability – does the person I am attempting to depend on have the resources, whether tangible or intangible, to support me in my time of need? The fourth and most important variable is compassion. I must be convinced that the person I want to trust really cares about me and is intent on thoughtfully providing the exact kind and amount of support I need. Considering these variables, it seems that depending on someone else can be risky.

However, depending on God should be different. Although I realize that God is perfect and should not be rated against any manmade criteria, I have had to remind myself of how He deserves my immediate and absolute trust in and dependence on Him. For one, His knowledge is incomparable. He knows EVERYTHING!! – about every cell in my body, about every thought that crosses my mind, about every force in the universe that impacts my life. I don't need to describe or explain anything to Him. Secondly, His ability is absolute. *"He is, over all things, Able"* (2:20). *"When He decrees a matter, He says, 'Be' and it is!"* (3:47). So I never need to worry that He can't do something or that it would be hard for Him. With this knowledge I shouldn't be impatient or dissatisfied, because not only is God completely in charge of every situation, He is also perfectly wise. I can rest assured that He knows what He's doing and that He never makes mistakes. In fact, being God makes him automatically very deliberate and precise with His acts. With this analysis, it gets easier and easier to trust God and depend on Him for every big and little thing. And it should be enough. But there's more.

He cares about me. He cares about us. He describes Himself as "Lord of the Universe, the entirely Merciful, the especially Merciful." The word Lord (or Rabb in Arabic) has the connotation of one who shelters, nourishes, protects, provides, educates, and shapes us. God says that He is *"closer to [each] one than his jugular vein"* (50:16) and that His mercy encompasses all things (7:156). Particularly for believers who do good, but not exclusively, He is Gentle, Loving, Forbearing, three of many qualities that He uses to describe Himself. And especially for the believers He promises His help: *"For helping the believers is ever incumbent upon Us"* (30:47).

So the variables in the trust formula are optimal for trusting God wholeheartedly and depending on Him utterly. What stops us? What stopped me?

For one, I was under the impression that I was knowledgeable and capable enough to be independent and self-reliant. But sometimes I am faced with a situation that is absolutely out of my control, that exposes my extreme vulnerability, that overwhelms and frightens me. One such incident was in 1990, when Iraq invaded Kuwait. It was a dangerous time for everyone in Kuwait, but as Westerners, my three children and I were particularly at risk. Eventually, we realized we had to leave, and decided that the safest route was through Iraq itself. The trip to Cairo and safety would have been nerve wrecking if I hadn't decided to *really* trust God, *really* depend on Him. And I did. Whenever fears nagged me, I said, *Trust.* When my strength waned, I said, *Depend on Him.* For eight days, as we inched our way to safety, living in our car, not knowing what lay ahead, I did not let worry take over. ***Trust!!***

He didn't let me down. For the first time in my life, I sensed the knowing, caring, supportive Presence by my side. Several small occurrences, although they may have appeared ordinary and coincidental to an outsider, proved to me that He meant what He said: "*And (He will) provide for him from where he has never conceived. Whoever relies on God – He will suffice him ….*" (65:3). Like the fact that just months before the invasion, we purchased a four-wheel drive vehicle and, for the first time in our lives, planned a summer road trip to Egypt; we researched the route, exchanged currency, and bought travel conveniences. Or like the chance interview with an international correspondent on the Jordanian border that my sister in the USA stumbled upon while channel surfing one night, which let the family know we were alive and well. Every day there were signs that God was watching over us. Most certainly, He's been there all the while, but I never leaned enough to feel His strong support. Now I know that I won't topple over when I lean toward Him.

Never has dependence felt so good. By relying on God, I have no doubt that my prayer will be heard, no fear that my need will go unmet, and no crushing feeling that the responsibility is mine and mine alone. What took me so long to trust my Creator's knowledge, ability and care, and to rely on Him absolutely? With this verse in mind, I can, in any circumstance, go forward: "*Say, 'Sufficient for me is God. There is no god but Him! I have put my trust in Him. He is the Lord of the Magnificent Throne*" (9:129).

Patience

"Are we there yet?" she asked for the tenth time. "Yes, dear, be patient." Two minutes later: "Are we there yet?" She thought she was being patient and I thought I was being patient. The concept is highly subjective, as each person's definition will depend on what stands in the way of instant gratification. I believe we may all naturally be impatient, in fact *extremely* impatient, which must be why patience is mentioned in the Quran as one of the qualities of someone who will go to Paradise. For example, *"I have rewarded them this Day [with Paradise] for what they have endured patiently; they are indeed the ones that are truly triumphant!"* (23:111)

Doesn't everyone have patience? We have to be patient to meet the requirements of our survival, to get along with people, to continue in our daily routines of work, chores and responsibilities, to carry out our duties to family and community, to restrain from indulging in things that we know will eventually harm us, and to face illness, aging and certain death, as well as occasional injury, loss, and calamity. Aren't we all compelled to be patient, whether we intend to or not? Is all patience the same? And what kind of patience merits Paradise?

I realize that we are not all compelled to be patient. We are free to choose patience or not. If we choose patience, then we are accepting to be governed by the requirements of success, tolerance, cooperation, moderation, balance, and common sense. To be governed by these principles means we must learn the rules of life and how to succeed in its different aspects. It takes a lot of hard work, but the eventual outcome usually includes a degree of physical comfort and enjoyment, fulfilling relationships, health, order, and beauty in our surroundings, optimism and mental health. Patience in life leads to good results.

If we don't adopt the kind of patience described above, we will endure (patiently or not) a life that is full of unpleasant consequences. If we are too lazy to work for a comfortable standard of living, our patience will be in the form of suffering a miserable existence. If we can't tolerate people who are different from us, we will have to be patient through contempt from others and isolation. If we indulge in unhealthy lifestyles, we should expect to suffer with disease. If we can't face our physical vulnerability and mortality, we trade patience for anxiety and depression. If we can't accept tragedy patiently, our losses will be replaced with panic, anger and grief. Instead of our life being filled with the fruits of proactive patience, it will be one of deprivation and despair.

These seem, to me, common-sense facts about patience. It shows that all patience is not the same. One kind involves working for a goal, the other is suffering through the consequences of irresponsibility. And because we are not perfect, we have all experienced both types. But is it enough? What kind of patience do the inhabitants of Paradise have?

As success in earthly life requires certain kinds of patience, so does Paradise; it requires two kinds of patience – one is proactive and the other reactive. The proactive type is striving to adopt a way of life approved of by God. It means making the effort to learn what God wants from us and then applying it in our lives. This will take determination and patience, but the reward is worth the effort. According to the Quran, *"The ones who fulfill the covenant with God and do not break its solemn pledge to Him, who keep joined all the relations and obligations that God has commanded to be joined and stand in awe of their Lord, and fear an evil reckoning, who endure with patience seeking the countenance of their Lord, who establish the prayer and spend charitably from what We have provided them, secretly and openly, and who avert what is evil with what is good... the angels will say, 'Peace unto you for that you persevered in patience! Now how excellent is the final Home!'"* (13:20-24). Those who repent, believe, do not bear false witness, pass by vile talk with honor, and heed the verses of God... *"those are the ones who will be rewarded with the highest place in heaven, because of their patient constancy"* (25:75). These verses show that the patience that merits Paradise involves a level of commitment and effort beyond the everyday patience of the common man.

The second kind of patience required for Paradise is reactive, and it is demonstrated by our reaction to things outside of our control, such as illness, injury, loss, calamity and all circumstances related to our physical vulnerability and mortality. The Quran guarantees us that *"And We will surely test you with something of fear and hunger and a loss of wealth and lives and crops, but give good tidings to the patient who, when disaster strikes them, say, 'Indeed, we belong to God, and indeed to Him we are returning'"* (2:155-156). Our reaction in adverse circumstances beyond our control should be to turn our thoughts to God, who describes Himself as wise, merciful, and caring. We should not disagree or be dissatisfied – as the Quran reminds us, *"He cannot be questioned as to what He does, while they will be questioned!"* (21:23). Instead, we should believe that God allowed such circumstances for our ultimate benefit. The Quran cautions, *"Perhaps you dislike something and it is good for you and perhaps you like something and it is bad for you. And God knows, while you know not"* (2:216). We must trust in God and His knowledge of the "big picture."

Both kinds of patience – making the effort to follow the way of life God envisions for us, and then truly submitting to God and His management of our lives – should have the characteristic of beauty. The Quran describes real patience as beautiful. *"Therefore, be patient with beautiful patience"* (70:5). Beautiful patience is one of contentment and absolute conviction of God's goodness and care. Beautiful patience is devoid of jealousy, resentment and despair. Beautiful patience is a reflection of a sound heart, one that is constantly tuned to God in gratitude and faith in ultimate good.

The requirements of patience for success in the mundane world are hard work and common sense, and the requirements of patience deserving of Paradise are striving for and submitting to God. However, even with this knowledge, some people will choose not to adopt patience. They will not wonder what God wants from them, nor will they care. They have no patience for things that disrupt their enjoyment of life and take a stance with God that is ungrateful and resentful. They risk facing God's censure, punishment, and exclusion from His mercy.

The encouragement we need is in the Quran itself: *"Indeed, mankind is in loss, except those who believe and do righteous deeds, and exhort one another to uphold truth and exhort one another to persevere with patience"* (103:2-3). *"Those who show patience and work righteousness – for them is forgiveness and a great reward"* (11:11). *"So persevere in patience, for the Promise of God is true!"* (40:77).

Love

I've been searching for love all my life. At first, I wanted to *be* loved – by parents, teachers, friends. I looked for proof that I was loved, never quite satisfied that what I witnessed was indeed the love I sought. As I raised a family, I became busy loving others in a million ways small and big, but deep inside I still did not understand this concept of love. I began to observe others' expressions of what appeared to be love. I read love poems, trying to fathom the mystery. I bought books – Rules of Love, Codes of Love, Languages of Love, the Art of Love – but rather than bring me closer to the real meaning of love, they raised more questions than they answered. There is something about love that, to me, was inexplicable.

Love is an innate and essential element in the makeup of our being in the sense that we all seek to love and be loved. Love may well be the driving force in everything we do – our love for ourselves, for others and for God will drive us moment by moment to certain behavior. I had to understand this most powerful emotion. What exactly is love? As a noun, it is an intense feeling of deep affection, admiration or delight for someone; as a verb, it is to feel or express that affection, admiration or delight. It describes a subjective emotion that is not always rational. It also describes a feeling that is often beyond one's control — hence, the phrase "falling in love."

Love is described in the Quran as something that God instills in our hearts. *"And of His signs is that he created for you from yourselves mates that you may find tranquility in them; and He placed between you affection and mercy"* (30:21). *"He has put affection between their hearts: if you had spent all that is in the Earth, you could not have produced that affection, but Allah has done it..."* (8:63). These verses imply that the feeling of love and affection for others originates from God and is a gift from Him. It is not something we can will in ourselves or create between people, which makes the feeling of love between people a sublime and blessed emotion.

Apart from loving others, people also love things, and these are mentioned in the Quran too. *"Man loves wealth with immense love"* (89:20). *"Man's love for wealth is intense"* (100:8). *"Beautified for people is the love for that which they desire – for women and children, heaped up sums of gold and silver, fine branded horses, and cattle and tilled land. That is the enjoyment of the worldly life..."* (3:14). Love for these things help us to become productive, cooperative people, but excessive love can make us become destructive and selfish. So, when it comes to loving things, we should exercise caution.

When I saw how the Quran ties love to virtue, my study of love became more interesting. *"You will never attain virtue until you spend something of what you love..."* (3:92) meaning when we give, we should give of the things we love. Another verse *"Whenever you speak, be just, even though it concerns a close relative"* (6:153) reminds us that our love for others should not make us do or say something unjust. Although I found no verse in the Quran that explicitly commands us to "Love one another," it does have many commands to **behave** as though we love one another, regardless of our feelings. *"Say kind words to people..."* (2:83); *"Pardon and overlook their misdeeds"* (5:13); *"Do not spy on one another, nor let any of you backbite others..."* (49:12); and *"... judge with justice..."* (5:42). It says that "The good deed and the evil deed are not alike. Repel (evil) by that which is better, and then the one between you and him is enmity will become as though he was a devoted friend" (41:34). Some verses are very specific in describing loving behavior: *"Your Lord has decreed that you should worship nothing except Him and show kindness to your parents; whether either or both of them attain old age, never say to them "Uf!" nor scold either of them. Speak to them in a generous fashion. Serve them with tenderness and humility..."* (17:23).

Aside from these Quranic verses, Prophet Muhammad advised his followers in innumerable traditions to be good to others. For example, although he could have simply said, "Love your neighbor as yourself," he took the time to describe the *behavior* of a loving neighbor: "Do you know what the rights of a neighbor are? If a neighbor seeks your help, extend it to him. If a neighbor asks you for a loan, lend him. If your neighbor becomes poor, then help him financially and attend to his poverty if you can. If your neighbor becomes ill, then visit him. If your neighbor is happy on certain gain, then congratulate him. If your neighbor is suffering a calamity, then offer him condolences. If your neighbor dies, then attend his funeral. Do not raise your building over his building, so that he would have no sun exposure or wind passage.

Do not bother your neighbor with the smell of your cooking, unless you intend to offer him some."[14] With these directives, I felt I was getting closer to understanding love.

Perhaps the Quran does not directly command us to "love one another" because we can't be expected to feel love for others unless there is some positive interaction (the verb). The feeling of love (the noun) is a **byproduct** of loving expressions (the verb). Instead, the Quran commands us to treat one another with justice, respect, forgiveness, patience, and kindness. By acting in this way, we can arouse the feeling of love for others in ourselves, and vice versa. Stephen Covey understood this well. As he explained in *The Seven Habits of Highly Effective People*:

> *In the great literature of all progressive societies, love is a verb. Reactive people make it a feeling. They're driven by feelings. ... Proactive people make love a verb. Love is something you do: the sacrifice you make, the giving of self ... If you want to study love, study those who sacrifice for others, even for people who offend or do not love in return. If you are a parent, look at the love you have for the children you sacrificed for. Love is a value that is actualised through loving actions. Proactive people subordinate feelings to values...*

I began to see that **true love** is principle-driven, not emotion-driven. Islam, through its instructions on love, insists on principle-driven love, a love that is proactive and action-based, not reactive and emotion-based. Love is an action, not a reaction.

Sometimes the requirements of love are too difficult, and in conflict with our own notions of love and happiness. But can we afford to neglect the demands of true love? How important is love? Muhammad, peace be upon him, said to his companions, "You will not enter Paradise until you have faith; and you will not complete your faith until you love one another." This love, although obviously based in principles and sometimes sacrifice, is tied to faith and eternal happiness – God's gifts to those who "walk the talk" of love.

---

14   Al-Tabarani 101

Perhaps I was getting closer to understanding love. I knew that if I treated others with kindness, forgiveness and generosity – acts of love – then feelings of love would arise, which would complete my faith and lead me to Paradise. Then the Quran gave a word of caution: *"Some people set up equals to God, loving them as they should love God. But those who believe have greater love for God..."* (2:165). My faith asks me to love others, but to love God most of all, as He is both the wellspring and objective of all expressions of love. With this in mind, I strove to make every interaction with others an act of love for my Creator. Loving others became easier and easier.

I loved as much as I could; I loved God most of all. Perhaps I had cracked the mystery of love. Then something extraordinary happened. I began to perceive love from others. Not the way I observed it before as an object of study, but I began to experience others' genuine love for *me*. At first I didn't see it, but it gradually dawned on me that I am loved by many people who tell me, show me, that they love me. Their words, actions and silent prayers touch me in profound ways. Suddenly I could see and feel love, loud and clear.

Love started as a question, became a quest, turned into work, was offered as worship, and then returned to me as a gift. It became a lens through which I see the world and through which the world sees me.

Prophet Muhammad, peace be upon him, said, "If Allah loves a person, He calls Gabriel, saying, I love so-and-so, O Gabriel love him.' So Gabriel would love him and then would make an announcement in the Heavens: 'Allah has loved so-and-so therefore you should love him also.' So all the dwellers of the Heavens would love him, and then he is granted the pleasure of the people on the Earth." By loving others, and being loved by them, I have felt God's love too. My lifelong search for love led me to God, where I found unexpected, mysterious, blessed love.

3

DEVOTION

3

Devotion

There comes a point when the seeker realizes that what he has been searching for is within reach. He can clearly see the final summit and gets ready for the steep climb. His focus is sharp, and his experience now pays off. A sense of purpose carries him forward to the object of his desire. Nothing can stop him now. Challenges, now considered minor obstacles or necessary lessons, are accepted, welcomed and appreciated as part of the journey. Progress, no matter how gradual or how difficult, is cherished as a step closer to the goal.

In this section I share my journey along the Divine Path and closer to the Divine Presence through acts of worship and aspirations of true submission to Him. My quest for God takes me to my innermost self and ends with a discovery of life, an understanding of love and a commitment to truth.

How do your paradigms and practices connect you to God and lead you closer to Him?

The Oases of Sinai

The Sinai Peninsula is breathtaking. During my many visits to Egypt I have taken several trips through Sinai to Hurgada, Sharm el-Shaikh, or Nuwaiba, home of the best coral reefs in the region. It is in Sinai that you can hear singing dunes, see turquoise waters, and stand in the shadow of towering desert mountains. You can visit the tombs of prophets, climb Moses' mountain and wonder about the site of the burning bush. No less impressive are the oases of Sinai – luxuriously green places in the starkness of sand and sky all around – and the people who live there, a few families coexisting as if they were the only inhabitants on Earth.

For years, as we drove through the peninsula, I marveled at the beauty and at the sacred history of the location. I would be deep in thought, meditating on its significance, when suddenly I would spot an oasis in the distance, and immediately feel a jolt of confusion and distress. There was something profound in the oasis with its simple people, something I couldn't understand, something I couldn't even express in the form of a question or problem. This continued for many years. Each time I would pass by bewildered, as the issue escaped me.

Then one summer I realized the source of my disquiet. I looked at the people there and realized that they live in utter isolation and seeming insignificance. This presented somewhat of a problem to me, since it clashed with the ideals and principles I was raised with. As an American girl born during Kennedy's presidency, I was taught, "ask not what your country can do for you, ask what you can do for your country." I was taught that each person has a contribution to make, and that the purpose of life is to "make a difference." I grew up searching for my calling and wondering how I would make a positive change in the world. It was a concept that permeated my outlook and influenced how I thought about life.

I've been a Muslim for a long time and well aware of the "purpose of life" according to the Quran: God said, "*I have created jinn and men to worship Me*" (51:56). And yet, I was unsettled by life in an oasis. I soon realized that these people challenged my deep-seated beliefs that we are all here to do something useful. What if someone wasn't useful? What if the resources, relations, or opportunities he had were not sufficient for him to enact positive change in the world? What if he merely survived, living day to day, and then died. Was his existence useless? Was he a mistake? Was it his fault? What was the purpose then, of his life? And by extension, what was the purpose of *my* life?

I thought long and hard about the verse, "*I have created jinn and men to worship Me.*" I thought about living in a modern city, and I thought about the people in the oases. About people on islands and in forests, about nomads, prisoners, and hermits. "*I have created jinn and men to worship me.*" We were not created to enact good – God is He who enacts good, sometimes through us. But we were created to worship God and to devote ourselves to Him. And I wondered, what is worship? How can people from such varied locations and manners of living realize their purpose, the purpose of their creation, which is worship?

Again, the Quran had the answer. It tells us how to worship our Creator:

With remembrance: "*I have chosen you, so listen to what is revealed. I am God [alone]! There is no god but Me, so serve Me and keep up prayer to remember Me by.*" (20:14)

With gratitude: "*He is the One Who has furnished you with hearing, sight, and intellect; yet seldom are you grateful.*" (23:78)

With glorification: "*Have you not seen how everyone in Heaven and Earth glorifies God, even to the birds lined up in flight? Each knows its prayer and how to glorify Him. God is Aware of whatever they do.*" (24:41)

With supplication: "*He is the Living; there is no deity except Him, so appeal to Him sincerely, making religion exclusively His. Praise be to God, Lord of the Universe!*" (40:65)

With obedience: "*Say, I have been forbidden to serve those you appeal to instead of God, since clear proofs have reached me from my Lord, and I have been ordered to commit myself to obey the Lord of the Universe.*" (40:66)

With love: "*Yet there are some people who adopt partners beside God whom they love just as they should love God. Those who believe are firmer in their love of God.*" (2:165)

With reliance on Him: *"If God supports you, there is no one who will overcome you; while if he should forsake you, who is there to support you? On God should believers rely."* (3:160)

With total dedication: *"Say, 'My prayer and my devotions, my living and my dying, all belong to God, Lord of the Universe; no partner has he; with that I am commanded, and I am the first of the Muslims (i.e., those who submit to Him).'"* (6:163)

If the purpose of life is worship, and if remembrance, gratitude, glorification, supplication, obedience, love, reliance, and total dedication are parts of worship, then the Arabs in Sinai could fulfill the purpose of their lives completely. And so could the people on islands and in forests, as well as nomads, prisoners, and hermits. And if someone without the resources, relations, and opportunities to enact positive changes in the world could at least worship his Creator, then he would have lived fully, and he would be significant to the only Power that really matters. I realized that mere survival with worship is meaningful, yet "changing the world" without worship has no lasting value.

And so when I pass by the oases of Sinai, I feel content that among them are people who worship God and live full, rich lives because of it. And interestingly enough, I realized that the lives of simple people in the isolated oases of Sinai made a difference.

Who Is God?

Human conceptions and imagery about God are mostly conjecture. The Quran says that we cannot comprehend God, that He is *"high exalted above anything that people may devise by way of definition"* (6:100) and that *"there is nothing like Him"* (42:11). Which makes me wonder, how can I understand God and how can I sincerely appreciate Him? To rely on my own perception of Him is as faulty as idolizing an actor for his role in a movie, and claiming to know the person behind the persona – I actually know very little about him. I deceive myself if I appreciate someone I don't really know. The only way to truly appreciate God, truthfully and sincerely, is to learn more about His attributes. But how can I learn more about God, without depending on conjecture or my own conceptions? There is only one way – to know Him from Himself.

I turn to the Quran, God's speech to mankind, to see what God says about Himself. Here, I find many names by which he describes Himself,[15] such as The Holy, The Majestic, The Almighty, The One, The Unique, The Loving, The Source of Peace, The Protecting Friend, The All-Knowing, The Wise, The Guide, The Resurrector, The Reckoner, The Avenger, The Equitable. God's names show His absolute power and control over all things, including evil. God is the perfection, the source, and the dispenser of all virtue and authority, as well as the source of all good.

Reflecting on the names of God and their implications has helped me navigate through life. Knowing that His knowledge is complete, I try to keep within God's stated limits and accept God's will when things go wrong, despite my best effort. Knowing that God's power is absolute, I do my best while depending on God for my needs and calling on Him exclusively. I feel reassured and comforted in times of distress. Knowing that God is both just and merciful, I avoid what could anger Him and hope for His forbearance and forgiveness when I make mistakes. Knowing that God is loving and wise, I feel cared for and particularly

---

15   According to a hadith from Prophet Muhammad, there are 99 names of God, which He has revealed in the Quran either as a name or in meaning. They help us understand His attributes and enable us to worship Him more fully.

blessed. I know that God's choices for me are best, which gives me confidence. If harm comes my way, I know it is because there is a purpose behind it and it is for my ultimate good.

I want to experience God in my life, and seek ways to connect with Him. The Quran says that some prophets experienced God by hearing His voice, such as Moses: *"And when he came to it [the burning bush], he was called, 'O Moses, indeed I am your Lord...'"* (20:11-12). Or God may send an angel, such as to Zachariah: *"The angels called out to him while he was standing in prayer... 'God gives you the good news of [a son] John, who will come to confirm a Word from God...'"* (3:39). Or He may send revelation or inspiration: *"And thus We have revealed to you (O Muhammad) an inspiration of Our command..."* (42:51).

However, I'm not a prophet so, as a regular person, I can expect to experience God through His revealed scripture, which is His message to us – to me – in human language. The Quran says, *"You receive the Quran directly from One who is All-Wise, All-Knowing"* (27:6). Another way I can experience God is through prayer, which is conversation with God. The Quran says, *"If my servants ask you about Me, I am near. I answer the call of the caller when he calls on Me"* (2:186).

Finally, I can experience God by striving to adopt His attributes in my struggle for personal and social perfection. For example, when I forgive, I experience something of the infinite forgiveness that comes from "The Forgiving." When I defend others, I experience some of the infinite guardianship that comes from "The Protector." When I am honest, I experience something of the Truth that has "The Truthful" as its source. I can experience God's divine names (His Being) as a recipient of others' goodness and as a doer of good. But in order to experience God to my fullest capability, I have to acknowledge the source of goodness. Virtue without God-consciousness seems defective and incomplete.

The Quran says that God has inspired every soul with knowledge of right and wrong, and that if I ignore and turn away from that inner voice I will lose touch with it, becoming spiritually blind and deaf. So I try to remember God by His beautiful names, and act upon virtues based in His names. I believe that if I remember God as I eat, work, rest, play and cry, then He will guide me. I will be grateful for every gift and patient with all adversity because I know He is good and merciful, that

He is aware of my every need, and that He truly knows what is best for me and my spiritual development.

God has honored us with knowledge of Him, and has given us the opportunity to connect with him minute by minute through reflection, prayer and action. Moreover, He has given us the gift of life and the privilege of worshipping Him. He has given us the gift of Himself and the possibility of being near Him for eternity. I can't imagine refusing such a generous invitation.

The Opening Chapter

When we meet someone new, we usually introduce ourselves with our name and a relevant role. "Hello, my name is Teresa. I'm a teacher."

Likewise, when God sent His message, the Quran, He provided an appropriate introduction in the first lines: His name, His title, and His role. *"In the name of Allah, the Continually Merciful, the Especially Merciful. All praise is for Allah, Lord of the Universe, the Continually Merciful, the Especially Merciful...."*

People use many words to refer to the Lord of the Universe such as God, the Great Spirit, the Divine, the Deity, the Higher Power, Nature, and so on; the list is endless if we consider the nomenclature for God in different languages and throughout history. It may not be incorrect to use these words, but they are *descriptions* of Him – titles we humans have conceived to identify him. However, the Lord of the Universe introduced Himself with *His name*, getting quite personal with me, the reader. *My name is Allah.* And in case I am apprehensive about being addressed by the Lord of the Universe, He immediately adds "the *Continually Merciful, the Especially Merciful.*" Now I am at ease. Any images of an angry, vengeful, or chastising Lord are overshadowed by His use of the word *merciful* four times in the first ten words of His message.

After introducing himself by His name and describing His prominent quality of ongoing and exceptional mercy, God shares with me His title: Lord of the Worlds.[16] While the word *lord* in contemporary English denotes a superior ruler, leader or officer, its meaning in the Quranic context must be examined in light of the Arabic word used, *Rabb*, which is commonly translated as Lord. The word Rabb in the Semitic languages can mean nourisher, one who provides the means of sustenance, one who raises or teaches another, one who serves as master over another, and, of course, God. In the Quranic context, the meaning combines these concepts to denote one who sustains and leads something through developmental stages so that it can attain its full stature or potential. The title Allah uses for Himself is "Lord of the Worlds," or

---

16   Worlds may refer to those we know (e.g., plants, animals) or to supernatural worlds of angels and jinn, or to ones we are unaware of.

of all beings, is followed again by the double qualifier—*the Continually Merciful, the Especially Merciful*. Not only is Allah He who nourishes, guides, and develops us, He does so with continual and exceptional mercy.

The verses continue: *"King (or Owner) of Judgment Day."* Just when I've started getting comfortable with the idea of a merciful Lord, Allah shares another of His titles with the reader. Suddenly I am jolted from a complacent existence under the provision and guidance of a continually and especially merciful Lord to a *Day of Judgment*, over which Allah, the King, will preside. The phrase implies not only an afterlife but also a trial. I become anxious. Judgment? How will I be judged? What is the criteria of success? What will happen next? I am dazed. At this point, there is a pause, and Allah invites the reader to respond. What should I say?

What does one say upon meeting the Lord of the Worlds and the King of Judgment Day? Common rules of etiquette between people do not necessarily apply. One would naturally be at a loss for words. So Allah provides the appropriate response for the reader: *"It is You we worship and it is You we ask for help. Guide us to the straight path, the path of those upon whom You have bestowed favor, not of those who have evoked your anger or of those who are astray."*

With this suggested response, Allah indirectly makes few points. First, that I should acknowledge Allah as the Lord, both in the sense of the only deity to be worshiped and of a benefactor whose assistance should be sought. Second, that I should offer the request in the collective sense, not a personal one, which would smack of selfishness; we are responding to the Lord as a community. Third, it is on Judgment Day that the community will be divided into those who have been favored by Allah, those who have evoked His anger, and those who have been lost. Fourth, there is hope: there is a straight path that leads to the envious position of being favored by Allah on Judgment Day. The suggested response is a request for guidance that, in turn, anticipates a reply.

It is given in the verses that follow the opening chapter. *"This is the Book [of Allah]; there is no doubt about it. It is guidance for Godfearing (or God-conscious) people..."* (2:2). Ever generous, the Lord sent an entire book of guidance, His message to the human community, which is known as the Quran. It thoroughly introduces the Creator to its reader and shows us how we are supposed to respond to Him.

After God introduces Himself in such a beautiful way, I look for guidance on how I am to react. Feeling it's impossible to express my love for God with thought and emotion alone, I want to respond in a concrete way and in a particular context. The Quran informs me of both particular deeds and the required context – His prescriptions and prohibitions achieved through personal conduct and interactions with others. Whether alone or among my community, I can express my love for God with acts of devotion to Him and by being both kind and just with others. With the hope of being counted among those upon whom *the Continually Merciful, the Especially Merciful* God bestows His favor, I'll do my very best.

Finding Peace

One of the most difficult times of my life was after the birth of my fourth child, when I suffered from post-partum depression. Like many kinds of hardship that leave us broken, healing involved a process of deep reflection, reevaluation, and recommitment. It was a slow and painful process but I worked through my perception of self, my choices in life and my relations with others. While struggling forward amidst heavy responsibilities and a weak support network, I eventually reached a state of peace and contentment.

My friend Janet, unknowingly, helped me through this painful period of my life when she gifted me with a set of 30 cassette tapes – the entire Quran, audible, one verse at time, first in Arabic then in English. During my drive time, which amounted then to almost three hours a day, I played the tapes. Knowing absolutely no classical Arabic when I started, I concentrated on the words to match the meanings between languages. After two years of daily lessons, I understood enough to switch to the only-Arabic recitation of the Quran, and continued learning for another year as I drove and then researched at home the new vocabulary. Eventually, I could understand fairly well the eloquent expressions of God's speech to man, and I was able to listen to the entire Quran at least once a month. This process transformed me.

When I listen to the Quran, God talks to me. He tells me how to live well, He describes Paradise, He teaches me little prayers, He tells me that He hears and knows everything in my heart. He tells me that He is merciful and kind, and that He helps and supports particularly those who believe in Him and treat others well. He teaches me, through stories of prophets, how I should approach life and how He chooses the very best for us, even if it meant prison for Joseph, exile for Abraham, and false accusations for Mary.

I came to the realization that He chose everything for me because it was best for me. I often used to think that if only I had been given more opportunities as a child, I could have been such a better person. But then I realized how my childhood made me strong, so it was good. Now I accept that everything I go through is carefully measured so that I can be my best self. When I am suffering, I ask, "What am I supposed to learn?" hoping that enlightenment will lessen the pain. Sometimes it means I have to change. Sometimes it means I have to forgive. Sometimes it means I have to stand up with confidence and self-worth, or set important boundaries. Some things I may never know. But I stopped questioning God.

I stopped doubting God's love and now I am sure of it. I feel it, and I can tap into it when I need to. Often I can stop the confusion to feel the embrace of my Creator, and experience His mercy and His limitless gifts. I know that if I don't feel God's love, it is because I have turned away from it, and I can just as easily turn again towards it, and recharge my soul with His love. It is so overwhelming sometimes, and it makes every created thing pale in comparison – they are shadows compared to the True Reality of God.

When I feel that warm embrace, and the security and confidence that I am being cared for in the best of ways, I can enjoy the smallest of things. I find more joy in my desert surroundings now than I ever did living on the shores of Lake Michigan, because now I feel God's love in it all. For example, when I saw a tiny flower growing out of a thin crack in desert rock, I felt it was created just for me to enjoy – what other purpose did it have? In that moment, I felt God was smiling at me, and I could not help smiling back.

When I remember the dark days of my depression, I feel sad for a moment. But then I realize how much I grew from that experience, how much more I empathize with others' struggles, and how I much more appreciate the smallest of miracles in everyday life. In many ways, depression was the beginning of the best days of my life. Having been at my lowest point, rising up was the only path available. Having been broken open, turning to my heart's Creator was the only way to mend. I learned, with certainty, that with hardship is ease. And I finally found peace.

Discovering the Quran

My first Quran was the 1934 translation by Abdullah Yusuf Ali. With English and Arabic text side by side, plus ample commentary, it was a good introduction to the Muslims' holy book. However, I didn't find it an easy read. I could not get a sense for its structure, and the verses seemed unorganized and fragmented. I struggled to complete reading its 114 chapters with over 6000 verses and felt, at the end, that I needed to start over again. So I found a different translation and started over. The new translation was different from Ali's literary style, and featured only the English text, which made it difficult to cross-reference a verse or phrase with an Arabic speaker. By the time I finished reading the last verse, I realized that the Quran was not like any other book. Being of divine origin, it naturally exceeds human conceptions of organization and begs to be read, studied, reflected upon, and discussed.

There are dozens of translations of the Quran, and each translator brings to light the meanings he understood through his research and experience. The more translations I read, the more frustrated I became. Wanting to both understand the Quran's meaning more deeply and experience the oral recitations in Arabic, I decided to study the single Arabic version available – the original words of God dutifully preserved since its revelation some 1450 years ago. I undertook my study in stages. My first goal was to get a gist of the meaning so that I could follow the Arabic recitation in the mosque or over the radio. Having accomplished that, I studied the words, one by one, and penciled in my translation on the pages. By then, I had a fair understanding of the basic meaning in Arabic. My next goal was to read the Arabic text and so I would listen to recordings while moving my finger along the Arabic script, which was later followed by the study and practice of pronunciation. After years of study, I had surpassed my original goal and was able to understand, read, and recite the Quran.

My experience with the Arabic Quran was vastly different from the English translations I had read. The Quran is an Arabic-language literary masterpiece both technically and aesthetically, making it impossible to translate the rhythm, rhyme, depth of denotation, and subtlety of connotation. The oral recitation is deeply moving, often bringing the listener to tears for its beauty and impact. With regular reading, I began to experience a pattern of different emotions as I progressed through the Quran. The first third is tiring to me and demands my focused attention to detail. The second third is easier to read and appeals to my philosophical, contemplative nature. Gradually, the text becomes more powerful. The sentence structure grows increasingly short and terse, the vocabulary more rich, the rhyme more obvious. The intensity of expression lends a sense of urgency to the text and evokes strong emotions like awe, humility, tension, anxiety, hope and longing. My turbulent emotions peak near the end, which is followed by a calm resolution that stems from three commands on the very last page that set me again on a clear and tranquil path: "Say He is Allah the One!... say I seek refuge in the Lord of daybreak...say I seek refuge in the Lord of mankind...."

This pattern of emotions intrigued me, which led me to a more in-depth study of the Quran's subject matter. The first third has long chapters and long verses, but the structure is simple and clear. It is first and foremost a call to pure monotheistic faith and declares in very clear terms that there is only one God, the Creator of all. It outlines the main acts of worship – strict monotheistic belief, prayer, fasting, charity and pilgrimage – and gives a blueprint for building an Islamic community. It includes instructions related to marriage and family life, diet, spending, inheritance, and caring for vulnerable sectors of society. It emphasizes justice and moderation. This section also discusses principles of war and peace, defense and peace treaties, and *jihad*, which is the ongoing struggle to remove obstacles to justice and peace. The first third is an indispensable handbook for balanced personal and communal life.

The second third of the Quran seems to focus more on natural, historic and spiritual phenomena that build faith in God's power, control and wisdom. My attention was drawn to natural phenomena such as the origin of the universe and the significance of water in creation (21:30), the creation and development of the embryo (23:14), the properties of milk and honey (16:66,69), the underground structure and purpose of mountains (16:15), the language of ants and birds (27), deep seas and interior waves (24:40), barriers between fresh and salty water (25:53), thunder (13:13) and sleep (39:42), all of which point to a Single Creator and Lord of the universe. Among the familiar things of this world, an unseen reality is also described, including angels, devils, Paradise and Hellfire – things we realize are not beyond the ability of an all-powerful Creator. Here the purpose of our earthly life is revealed – a test of faith and deed – and the inevitability of judgment and recompense is emphasized.

This section also mentions many miracles, such as the story of Prophet Muhammad's night journey to Jerusalem and ascension to the Heavens, the story of several youth who slept for 300 years. It describes the miracles of Moses – the staff, his hand, the Red Sea – as well as those of Jesus, including his immaculate conception and his ability to cure the sick and raise the dead, all by God's permission. All of these subjects, which range from history to the Hereafter, from natural phenomena to nature-defying miracles, from the purpose of this life to what awaits us in the next, call me to faith and goodness.

The last third of the Quran, like the first, has prescriptions for the faithful but they lean toward personal behavior rather than family, commercial or military matters. For example, chapter 49 forbids slandering others, looking down on others, spying on one another, backbiting, defamation and suspicion. Many verses urge us to refine and perfect our character and behavior, and remind us of God's justice, which manifests when we face the consequence of our own choices. Key verses are *"No bearer of burdens shall bear another's burdens"* (53:38), *"On that day you will be exposed; not a secret of yours will be hidden"* (69:18), and *"Shall we treat those who believe and do good works as those who spread corruption in the Earth; or shall we treat the pious as the wicked?"* (38:29). Complementary verses describe in alternation the punishment of ingrates, unrepentant sinners, and those heedless of God's warnings, and the relief and reward of those with firm faith and wholesome work. Descriptions of Paradise are particularly enticing.

When I read the Quran as a whole, I am taken on both a rational and emotional journey that is not unlike the experience of being engrossed in a skillfully crafted novel, or a beautifully orchestrated symphony, or a brilliantly produced film. The integrity, meaning and nuance of the verses impact me each time in similar ways and yet differently, depending on my frame of mind or current events in my life. Awestruck at its brilliance and beauty, I am thankful for the privilege of my journey with the Quran. Every step on the path, whether reading a translation of the meanings, or delving into a dictionary in painstaking study, or donning headphones for enraptured listening, is an experience with the Divine Speech. I have found nothing in life as enriching, as satisfying, as beautiful. It's the discovery of a lifetime.

Islamic Art

I love Islamic art – the calligraphy, the arabesques, and especially the geometric and symmetric patterns created from lines and circles. I am fascinated by the infinite variations of line-and-curve repetitions that are possible with just a compass, ruler, and pen. Having dabbled in what I call "art for non-artists," I am humbled by the vision, technical accuracy and patience that are required to produce an even remotely impressive, half-page piece.

The design always begins with a single point on a page or canvas. It is from this point that a line or circle is first drawn, and from which a work of art takes shape. Without that point of reference, without the consideration that each line and curve originates from that point, and without respect for the relation that every intersecting point has with the original one, the whole pattern will be imperfect, uneven and eventually unrecognizable.

Islam, as the inspiration for this beautiful art form, is identical in that it, too, has a single point from which every thought, intention, and action begins. That point of reference is God. When someone makes God the single reference point in his life, from which all expression originates, his life can be one of both technical precision and artistic beauty, of both strict discipline and joyful creativity. In Islamic art, the original point is simply a dot on a page. In Islamic culture, a single, unique God is the focal point, around which all of life revolves.

God is described in the Quran as *al-Samad, the Eternal One to whom all instinctively turn with their pleas*, which highlights our innate recognition of and need for a deity, a need most appropriately satisfied in the worship of God. However, when God is not worshipped, other things fill the vacuum. Some people fill their need for God by preoccupying themselves with physical pleasures, romantic love, earning and spending, youth and beauty, status and titles, or blatant power and domination. The Quran asks, *"Have you seen the one who takes as his god his own desire?"* (25:43). In a truly God-centered life, however, the goal is to please our Creator, which begs the question, "what does God want?"

The Quran states clearly the purpose of this temporary, earthly life: *"[He] created death and life to test you [as to] which of you is best in deed...*" (67:2). The framework and methodology is specified: "*And We will certainly test you with something of fear and hunger and a loss of wealth and lives and fruits...*" (2:155-156). "*...and We test you with evil and with good as trial...*" (21:35). The criteria is identified: "*And by the soul and He who fashioned it, and informed it with consciousness of its wickedness and its righteousness, truly, whoever purifies it (causes his soul to grow) has succeeded and whoever defiles it (stunts its growth) has failed.*" (91:7-10) And the consequences are forewarned: "*...every soul may be compensated for what it has earned, and they will not be wronged.*" (45:22). These verses indicate that the purpose of life on Earth is spiritual growth, which is enhanced by a variety of both favorable and adverse situations that are designed to enable us to realize our spiritual potential.

But personal growth cannot occur in a vacuum. There must be a context: families, neighbors, colleagues, strangers – both good and bad people – which comprise our communities that, together, span the whole of humanity. Just as geometric shapes intersect and overlap to create an Islamic design, individuals and peoples interact and collaborate to build a global society. While individual success may be easy to achieve, building an effective and cohesive society is not. To facilitate this challenge, God has provided a wholesome code of conduct that covers spiritual, personal, social, political, economic, and legal areas of life, enabling not only individual citizens but also society at large to achieve their potential.

This code of conduct addresses every aspect of civil life. It comprises personal practices that protect faith, health and intellect. It recommends family conduct that facilitates a wholesome and equitable lifestyle for each member, and social ethics that promote decency and solidarity. It outlines welfare measures that protect and provide for the weak and vulnerable, as well as civil and executive duties that ensure justice, prevent oppression, and meet the needs of the people. It recommends business practices that encourage economic development and wealth distribution, and directs international relations and principles of defense to ensure peace and security in a multicultural, religiously diverse world. This divinely-based legislation aims to protect individual citizens while promoting universal prosperity and social stability. It provides a benchmark for success that is based in the wisdom and care of our Maker.

The characteristic feature of the divine law that is designed to regulate our social, political, and economic activities is moderation. Prophet Muhammad emphasized the importance of moderation by repeating three times, "*Ruined are those who insist on hardship in matters of religion!*"[17] and God Himself said that He "*has not placed upon you in the religion any difficulty*" (22:78). All forms of extremism are discouraged in Islam, including both extravagance and austerity. The Quran says, "*God intends for you ease, and He does not want to make things difficult for you*" (2:185). Many verses promote moderation such as "*Eat and drink but do not waste; certainly He does not like the extravagant*" (7:31) and "*And those who, when they spend, are neither extravagant nor stingy, but hold a medium (way) between them*" (25:67).

God offers us the opportunity to create both beauty and balance in our personal lives and in our communities. We are required to consistently refer to the central point of measurement, which is divine guidance. To deviate from that framework is to jeopardize personal and social integrity and stability. But with discipline and patience, we can each achieve both. Each of us can express our own individuality in unique lives that are full and meaningful and, at the same time, we can unite and cooperate with others to build mutually supportive and synergistic communities. The result, like a mural of tessellating Islamic art, has infinite proportion and possibility.

As we produce our masterpiece, whether a vibrant drawing or a thriving community, we will be faithful to that single point where order and beauty originated. We will also realize that producing anything of value takes time and requires patience. But we know it can be done.

We are all artists.

---

17   Muslim. Riyad as-Salihin 144.

My Prayer

When I hear the call to prayer, I feel a personal invitation to meet God. *Allahu Akbar! God is Greatest!* The meeting with Him is certainly more important than whatever I'm doing, but there is a generous window of time in which to perform the prayer, so I do so at my earliest convenience. I want to be first to answer the call, not one of the laggards, or one who prays randomly, only when the mood strikes. I want to be one of the regulars. The prayer call entices me. *Come to prayer! Come to success!*

In anticipation of my dialogue with God, I prepare myself and my surroundings. Just as I would groom for a meeting with an important dignitary, I carefully groom myself, starting with ablutions. The ritual ablution begins with *Bismillah. In the name of God.* Washing hands, face and feet serves as a transition from the temporal to the transcendent. I brush my teeth if possible, as my words are received by angels and carried to the Heavens. I then wear dignified clothes for this encounter with God, most conveniently a robe that reveals only my hands and face. I choose a place to pray that is clean and without distractions, and I often use a small rug for this purpose, which then becomes my personal, sacred space to be with God. I face the Kaabah, the first house of worship on Earth and the unifying direction of the Muslims' prayer. The mindfulness of these preliminaries prepares me for an intimate dialogue with God, for He says that He not only hears us – both our audible words and inaudible thoughts – but also answers us.

Allahu Akbar, God is the Greatest. I have entered into the prayer. Now I will focus on graceful postures and deliberate words, resisting unnecessary movement and distractions that come to mind. With hands folded across my chest, I say the *Fatihah* or opening chapter of the Quran.[18] *Praise be to God... it is You alone we worship, and from You alone we seek aid. Show us the straight way, the way of those you have blessed... Amen.* I recite some verses of the Quran I have learned, focusing on the meaning of the words He has given us.

---

18   Ritual prayers are performed in Arabic, enabling the worshipper to join congregational services anywhere in the world and giving him the incentive to learn basic Arabic, the shared language of Muslims.

Now I bend forward, making my body a right angle, with my hands on my knees. I stretch my back flat, keeping my face parallel to the ground. *How perfect is my God the Magnificent.* I show my subservience and proclaim His grandeur. Then I return to a perfectly vertical standing position for a moment as I say, *God hears those who praise Him... Our Lord, and for you is Praise.*

Now I drop down, back straight, until my knees reach the ground, then I put my hands down and then my face on the ground. My fingers and toes face forward to the Kaabah, each part of my body participating in worship. *How perfect is my Lord the Most High*, I whisper as I prostrate. My limbs, my voice, my mind, my heart all prostrate. Then I sit up momentarily, calm. *My Lord, forgive me.* Then I prostrate again. *How perfect is my Lord the Most High.*

Then, using the strength of my legs, I gracefully erect myself tall and straight, saying *Allahu akbar, God is the Greatest*, before beginning another cycle from the beginning.[19] With each repetition, the prayer becomes more fluid. When I have completed them, I sit for the final supplication, which includes salutations to God, prayers of peace for the pious servants of God, and blessings on Prophets Muhammad and Abraham, and their people.

Humbly, I offer my personal petitions for myself and my loved ones, for guidance and forgiveness, for the best of this life and the best of the Hereafter. Then I offer greetings of peace to my right *As-salaam alaikom wa rahmatullah, Peace be upon you, and the mercy of God,* and the same to my left. I may sit now quietly, if I have time, for reflection, gratitude, or further praise.

After engaging in the routine and mundane activities of life, my connection with God weakened or lost, I return, five times a day, to the sacred place of prayer. I have established this spiritual routine patiently and persistently, which is now as natural as my physical routines like eating three meals and exercising daily.

In addition to the ritual prayer, I informally communicate with God throughout the day with spontaneous prayers from the heart – in times of need, in moments of joy, during reflection or strenuous

---

19   The dawn prayer has two cycles, the two daytime prayers have four cycles, the
      dusk prayer has three cycles, and the night prayer has four cycles.

effort. Prophet Muhammad set a perfect example by supplicating often from the time he woke up until he slept at night. His supplications were recorded by his companions and touch every aspect of life – from the usually mindless activities such as dressing in the morning to the most serious and somber situations like preparing a body for burial.

To worship God with a combination of ritual prayer and supplication is the most exalted occupation I aspire to, one that requires only a few minutes for each of the five daily prayers and a presence of mind at other times. It does not require me to isolate myself from worldly endeavors, but rather to focus on a higher authority while engaging in them. It does not require me to abstain from physical pleasures but rather to express gratitude for the many blessings I enjoy. It does not require deep study and rigid exercise, but rather a sincere and tender heart, ever mindful of the Creator. As the Quran instructs us, "*seek help in patience and prayer; it is indeed burdensome except for those of humble spirit – those who are mindful that they shall meet their Lord, and that they shall return to Him*" (2:45).

When my life gets too hectic, too distracting, or too intense, the prayer is there to calm and refocus me. And when my life becomes routine and monotonous, the prayer invigorates and inspires me. My prayer, when I turn with complete physical, mental and spiritual focus toward my Maker, is my pillar of strength and my source of comfort. I often find myself waiting for the next call to prayer when I can lose myself in the presence of God. I wait for that personal invitation – Come to prayer! Come to success! I am here, my Lord, I am here.

Ramadan Therapy

Modern life, which is characterized by computerization, communication, and globalization, is different from when I was a child. Information and communication technology has made work easier for some
and eliminated jobs for others; it has given us more leisure options but
has also kept us tied to the office no matter where we are. Although it
has the potential to connect and unite us, it has noticeably contributed
to some mental and social problems. "Modern man" is often characterized by lack of purpose, distraction, low stamina, isolation, loss of
community involvement, decreased empathy, and general depression.
Given the predominance of technology and increasingly hectic schedules, it's challenging to make major lifestyle changes. But our Creator
has prescribed a treatment for whatever social, emotional, or personal
challenge we face in life – it is called Ramadan.

Feeling a lack of purpose in your life? Fast the month of Ramadan. Nobody would undertake such a long and difficult commitment
without a reason, whether for religious conviction, health benefits, personal challenge, or solidarity with Muslims. The Quran says, "*Fasting
has been prescribed for you as it was prescribed for those before you so
that you may learn God-consciousness*" (2:183). If you sincerely fast, ob-
serving the restrictions on food, drink and intimacy in daylight hours,
you will develop a strong sense of purpose – which for most is to obey
and worship Almighty God. You will also become a more sincere person, since fasting cannot really be observed by another person – only
you and God. Ramadan is the perfect time to ask, "What is the purpose
of my existence?"

Most people nowadays are distracted due to busy schedules, in-
cessant phone messages and emails, and the demands of media for our
attention. We lack focus and can hardly finish one task from start to
finish without distractions. Some people cannot even eat a meal without their phones nearby so they can check their notifications. If this
describes you, I recommend fasting the month of Ramadan, which will
eliminate at least one major distraction in our lives – eating – during
daylight hours, which will increase productivity and focus on other activities. And then, when the meal is finally served after sunset, I guaran-
tee you will put your phone away so you can enjoy your food.

We generally have less physical strength and lower stamina than our parents and grandparents had at our age, due to our sedentary lifestyles and the prevalence of desk jobs. Fasting Ramadan will improve your fortitude and determination; how else would you be able to refrain from satisfying your basic needs and desires for such long periods? How else would you be able to ignore hunger, thirst and fatigue while you carry on with life's usual demands? Ramadan is a perfect time to show yourself what you're capable of. You will discover a self-disciplined, patient, flexible, and resilient person.

Another byproduct of our modern lifestyles is isolation. Families are often separated and must resort to social media to keep in touch. Social media has enabled us to have friends from around the world that we meet in virtual spaces. However, this has had a negative impact on the "in-person" relationships with those around us, with many people preferring to relate to others through their phones. Ramadan helps this situation because there are many communal meals, whether at home, in mosques, or special gatherings for social groups. In addition, the extra attention on prayer brings neighbors together in the mosques daily, which builds stronger communities. Finally, *zakat ul-fitr*, or the pre-holiday charity, requires us to reach out to someone less fortunate in the spirit of sharing and celebration.

Modern life can sometimes lead to apathy, which is caring little for others, and a sense of entitlement, which is overestimating your rights. Feeling the hunger and thirst of fasting makes you keenly aware of the blessing of food and clean water in your life, and more aware of the fact that many people do not have what you will promptly come to consider a luxury. Feeling the deprivations of the poor is a wonderful lesson in empathy and compassion, one that is never forgotten after fasting the month of Ramadan, and which makes it so much easier to share our resources with the disadvantaged.

Finally, all the above pitfalls of the modern man can lead to depression, which is common today. Fasting Ramadan is a way to start overcoming depression because it has several positive results simultaneously: a renewed sense of purpose, realizing your personal strength, increased involvement with others, awareness of blessings that you formally took for granted, taking control of yourself through managing your needs, desires, and thoughts, and drawing closer to your Creator and the Provider of all your needs.

Fasting throughout the month of Ramadan definitely has its benefits in this life, especially in the modern age. And this is just the tip of the iceberg, because there are well-researched medical benefits as well as deeply personal spiritual blessings, not to mention the promised rewards that ensue in the Hereafter. The total benefits of fasting are known only to God, who says in the Quran, "*... and it is better for you to fast, if you only knew*" (2:184).

Taking Control

It is not unusual to sometimes feel overwhelmed by the many responsibilities of modern life – family needs, work schedules, social commitments, and the pressure to develop professionally or face obsolescence. It is also not uncommon to lack focus because of the many forces that take our attention in different directions, such as the constant notifications of our social media accounts, the allure of online entertainment, the boredom that drives us to local attractions, and our own physical needs for food, enjoyment and rest. All of these pressures and distractions weigh us down, making it difficult to sift out our goals, focus on achieving them, and build the life we dream of.

Fasting is a great way to regain control of our lives. Both the proscribed annual fast of Ramadan and regular voluntary fasting throughout the year build discipline, stamina, and confidence. There are three levels of fasting. The basic level of fasting is to abstain from eating, drinking, smoking and intimacy during daylight hours. To do this for an entire month proves to me that no physical pleasure can control me; in fact, I take control of the food, the sugar, the caffeine, and all sensual pleasures. I prove to myself that I can control my impulses and regulate the physical demands of human life. This is not a small thing. And there's more.

I experience a second level of fasting when I abstain from saying what shouldn't be said and seeing what shouldn't be seen. I refrain from expressing anger, sharing gossip, telling little lies, and watching violence, gore, and sexual content on my screens. I realize that having control over my stomach is insignificant if I can't control my tongue, ears, and eyes. Exercising that kind of discipline for a month shields me from the problems I often bring upon myself when I say or do something spontaneously in reaction to others without pausing to consider the effects, or when I regularly experience what taints my best self. The second level of fasting empowers me to regulate the social and recreational aspects of my life. That is not a small thing! But there's more.

I experience a third level of fasting when I resist what is useless, negative, and mundane and replace it with what is constructive, positive, and beneficial. It's like cleaning my closet – getting rid of the clothes that are outdated, ill-fitting, worn out, or useless. Likewise, I purge my mind from old mindsets that hold me back, from ugly attitudes that accentuate my flaws, from excuses that keep me from being my best self and from worthless clutter that crowds my mind. This naturally extends to activities, as I reevaluate how I spend my time and whether it contributes to my ultimate success and happiness.

When I apply the three levels of fasting and really focus on the physical, social and mental benefits, I can finish the month of Ramadan possessing the tools I need to stay in control of my life. I am better able to control my body and mind, and I can focus my energy on achieving what really matters. I aim to emerge from this annual training with enhanced feelings of autonomy and self-determination, greater belief in my potential for goodness and meaning, and powerful tools to help me meet my goals for the coming year. And when I falter and forfeit some of that control, Ramadan will revisit next year, and every year, to reinforce its valuable lessons.

But before I credit myself with strength, autonomy, and potential, I must acknowledge the source of this beautiful month. Our Creator, who knows me inside out, has ordained this fast as a way to express my gratitude and become more conscious of Him. Practicing the three levels of fasting, whether during Ramadan or throughout the year with voluntary fasting, gives me the clarity, strength and incentive to stay focused on the terminal point of this journey called life, which is standing before my Creator with my record in hand. It is here – when my deeds, words and thoughts are on display – that I will be thankful for Ramadan, when I learned to take control.

Sharing

Sharing is one of our most basic, innate virtues. Seen even in toddlers, who spontaneously hand their food or toys to someone, it is a way to connect with others and share an experience. As we grow up, we are instructed to share because it is a way to make friends, or because we are to be fair, or just to share some happiness. Sharing, or charity, is a cornerstone of all great religions as well. In the Quran, mention of charity is usually coupled with prayer, the pair being the essence of the meaning of life: devotion to God and service to people.

Charity can be in the form of a random act of kindness, a spontaneous gesture whose purpose is to bring happiness to another person, expecting nothing in return. But more often, charity means voluntarily and intentionally giving assistance, typically money or goods, to those in need. These two kinds of charity – the random acts of kindness and the premeditated effort to help someone in need – are two types of charity that are promoted in Islam.

The first type is *"sadaqah."* In Arabic, the word for charity (*sadaqah*) is closely related to friend (*sadeeq*) and fidelity (*sidq*). So charity in the sense of *"sadaqah"* is to give, genuinely, in friendship, expecting nothing in return. Prophet Muhammad said, "Charity is due for every joint, in every person, on every day the sun comes up. To act justly between two people is charity; to help a man with his transport, lifting him onto it or hoisting up his belongings onto it, is charity; a good word is charity; and removing a harmful thing from the road is charity." Even a smile is considered charity. These spontaneous acts of charity show our connection to and concern for others.

The other type of charity in Islam is *"zakat,"* best translated as alms-tax. In Arabic, this word is related to growth, development, blessings, and purification. Different from the spontaneity of *"sadaqah,"* zakat is calculated annually against one's assets and allocated for specific recipients. Essentially a "rich man's tax," it is calculated according to different rates for minimum thresholds of different material assets. For example, *zakat* amounts to 2.5% of cash savings, 5-10% on crops (depending on labor intensity), and a portion of livestock. The cash, crops and livestock are then apportioned to specific categories of recipients such as deserving individuals, food banks, scholarship funds, debt relief and crisis management. The annual payment of *zakat* is one of the pillars, or main acts, of worship, in Islam. It upholds the principles and purposes of community, which is to enhance the quality of life and potential of each member.

With this distinction between spontaneous charity and deliberate alms-tax, I am able to share with others in the most meaningful ways. There are the daily niceties – smiling at the young mother and her child on the walk path, dropping a bill in the tip cup at the corner coffee shop, sending a homemade cake to a neighbor. All of these show others that I see them, I value them, and I think of them. Other gestures include an encouraging word to my student, a phone call to my mom, a warm embrace with my daughter. They show others that I believe in them, I love them, and I need them.

Charity can be collected through food drives or fund campaigns to meet ongoing or sudden shortages in a community. More often than not, giving is carefully thought out to reach those who need it most and in the most compassionate ways. Sometimes charity is secret – so secret that the recipient does not know who gave it – and sometimes it is in the open, which often encourages others to contribute to a cause. Whether spontaneous or planned, secret or open, each act of charity connects with others in concern and solidarity.

Potential recipients of "sadaqah" are everywhere. However, I have to search for recipients of the annual alms-tax, or *zakat*. I could give my annual dues to one of the many organizations that collect and distribute *zakat* to peoples suffering from natural disasters, famine, civil war, dislocation, or exploitation. But I prefer to reach individuals who may not be covered by such organizations. I have a network of friends and acquaintances who alert me when there is an eligible recipient of *zakat* – the destitute, debt-ridden, or deprived. I am able to help hand-to-hand and, sometimes, I can witness the effect of my dues.

Take Jenny, for example. My contact in the Philippines informed me that a 42-year-old man died, leaving behind his wife, Jenny, and six children. With medical bills, unpaid loans and daily expenses, she couldn't even afford to bury her husband. The first step was to wire money to bury the deceased, and to pay overdue bills and loans. I thought this would at least get Jenny and her children at a baseline for a decent life. Then I learned that the roof was leaking, and my contact sent pictures of their house. Except it wasn't a house, it was a shack made of scrap metal and wood, tied, hammered, and propped together. I appealed to family and friends who helped to renovate the structure so it would be safe and dry in the wet island weather, to finance a small grocery stall on the side of her house so that she could earn money, and to settle school fees for the children. Gradually, Jenny got back on her feet, blessed with unexpected funds to get her through her darkest days and with hope for a decent future for her and her kids. I stay in touch with her through my contact and am rewarded with photos of a happy family. Our *zakat transformed* them.

Another example is Denver. With an expired visa and mounting fines, he was trapped in a catch-22 situation. Because of the expired visa, he couldn't get a job, and, without a job, he couldn't pay the fines and renew his residency visa. He felt trapped, depressed, and hopeless. I learned of his situation and paid his fines so he could renew his residency. Later, by chance, I saw that he was job searching in a creative and optimistic way. The *zakat empowered* him.

These donations should not be admired in the least – that is not my intent in disclosing their details. *Zakat* is an *obligation* on the rich, who are defined as those who have had savings for an entire year. It is a privilege to be "rich" – rightfully defined as someone who has money in the bank – and it is our duty as brothers to lend a hand to those who struggle hand to mouth, day after day.

Having to calculate *zakat* is proof of the material blessings we often take for granted. Searching for recipients of *zakat* makes us aware of the many people in our communities who struggle. And paying *zakat*, year after year, is a way to build a habit of giving, and to oust greed from our hearts. It prevents us from the depravity of hoarding wealth while those around suffer in poverty. The Quran says, "...*spend. It is better for you. And whoever is protected from the stinginess of his soul – it is those who will be the successful.*" (64:16).

In Islam, *zakat* is required on material assets that are beyond our basic needs. But we would do well to think of all of our resources – home, belongings, car, time, knowledge, skills, etc. – and ask how can we give a portion of these to others. How can I use my varied resources to connect with others and share an experience? Whether it's to make friends, or because it's fair, or just to share some happiness, charity brings meaning to life. It empowers, strengthens, and uplifts both the receiver and the giver. It says that we are family, hand in hand, sharing an experience, sharing our abundance, sharing our love.

My Pilgrimage

I was among an estimated 2.5 million people who gathered in the holy city of Mecca in April 1997. We were there to perform the rites of the Hajj, or pilgrimage, to visit the first house of worship on Earth, the Kaabah, which was built by Abraham in ancient history, and which has continued to be the center of worship for the monotheistic religion of Islam. Awe and humility filled me as I witnessed pilgrims from every nation of the world gather to worship God, seek His forgiveness, and renew their commitment to Him. People of all races and cultures stood silent in perfect concentric rows during congregational prayer. Both the rich and the poor stood before God, supplicating with outstretched hands, and people of all ages and abilities strove their utmost to perfect their worship. I cannot express how grateful I felt to be among the Muslims in Mecca.

The rites of the Hajj originate in Abraham and his family, and were restored by Muhammad after being gradually distorted or lost in the interim. To be performed at least once in our lifetimes, if we are physically and financially able, the pilgrimage is not merely a religious obligation but also a rite of spiritual passage and a journey of self-discovery. While the modes of transportation and the standard of accommodation have changed across the centuries, the rituals have not. They remind Muslims of their ties to both ancient and modern Muslim communities, but more importantly of their ultimate death and return to God. As I began my pilgrimage, I put all worldly concerns out of my mind and prayed, in the words of Prophet Muhammad, "At Your service O Lord, at Your service. There is no god but You. All praise, goodness and authority are Yours. There is no god but You."

The essence of the Hajj is spending the day on the plain of Arafat near Mecca. It is said that on this day God descends to the lowest heaven and says, "Behold my servants who come tired and dusty in search of My mercy," and that He answers the prayers of His supplicants this day. Naturally, the whole day was spent in worship, prayers, and meditation. The hope of His presence, the longing for nearness to Him, and the promise of His Mercy were fuel for the heart and soul. Anxious glances at my watch reminded me how short a day can be and how precious time really is. As the sun set, I left Arafat, regretting that the day had ended so soon and longing for an eternal home in His presence.

After sunset we proceeded to Muzdalifa to rest before completing the Hajj the next day. There we collected pebbles, which we would later cast at the three pillars erected to symbolize Satan. This rite originates with Abraham who, on at least three separate occasions, confronted Satan, who sought to tempt him and lead him away from obedience to God. On one such occasion, Abraham understood God's wish for him to take his wife Hagar and infant son Ishmael to the barren, unpopulated valley of Mecca and leave them there. He did so and, as he walked away, Satan tempted him to return for them. Unflinching in faith, Abraham cast stones at Satan to drive him away. On another occasion, Abraham saw in a dream that he was to sacrifice his young son and understood that it was a command from God, a test of faith. Both Abraham and Ishmael were willing to obey, but Satan tried to tempt them. They cast stones at him to drive him away. As Ibrahim placed the knife at his son's throat, a ram appeared out of nowhere, and Abraham knew that it was sent as a substitute; he had proven his faith and his obedience. Thus, after casting pebbles at the pillars, the pilgrim sacrifices a sheep or other animal and distributes its meat to the poor, which is symbolic of faith, obedience and charity.

To complete our Hajj, we visited the Sacred Mosque in Mecca to perform seven circumambulations of the Kaabah.[20] Our revolutions around the House of God, like the prayer of Abraham and Ishmael as they built it, impressed upon me the purpose of life: *"Our Lord, accept this service from us and make us Muslims, bowing to Your will, and of our progeny a people bowing to Your will"* (2:128). We then walked seven times between the ancient hillocks of Safa and Marwa as Hagar did after being abandoned in the valley. She ran in frantic search for water for her infant son from one hill to the other until, after the seventh time, water sprang up at her son's feet. The underground spring, called Zamzam, has quenched the thirst of innumerable worshippers ever since.

---

20   Although seven is the number of circumambulations specified for the Hajj, the reason is not known. Muslims perform the rites of Hajj as symbolic acts that have bases in Abraham's tradition, and with faith in their divine purpose and significance.

We often drank from that spring with prayers for health and strength, for Prophet Muhammad said that in Zamzam water is both nutrition and healing power. With our Hajj complete, we thanked God for the opportunity and the means to fulfill our obligations to Him and prayed for His acceptance of our effort.

The rites of the Hajj replaced mere intellectual comprehension of religious history with the experience of sharing faith and practice with our ancient fathers. I developed profound respect and affection for Abraham and his family, and I felt immense pride in being one of his faith – a true monotheist. As millions of Muslims gathered on those days in worship, I felt a brotherhood that renewed my faith in the worldwide Muslim community and inspired hope for our future. Thus, the pilgrimage linked the past to the present and, through me and my fellow pilgrims, both ancient and future generations of Muslims were bound in faith and fellowship.

A few images of the Hajj are carved in my memory. An old man, smaller and thinner than I, brushed against me as we pressed through the crowded corridor on the way to the Sacred Mosque. He turned and implored, "Forgive me, pilgrim." Tears welled in my eyes as I forced a smile. He had done nothing to offend me. Being young and strong, I could only feel shame as he asked me for forgiveness. I remember him often and ask God to bless him.

And then there was Şeyma, a beautiful woman from Turkey, who stopped me in the market one morning and asked in broken English where I was from. She gave me a book and said, "*hadiya*," the Arabic word for gift. I was astounded by the feeling that this woman was my sister and my friend because of our faith and by the fact that the language of the Quran was our means of communication. My husband and I later met her husband, a member of the Turkish parliament, and learned that they have three children. They asked us to pray for them. That's all I know of Şeyma from Turkey, yet I feel an affinity with her that is symbolic of my affinity with all true Muslims around the world – one people who worship one God and mold their lives around faith and obedience, resulting in similar lifestyles and a common language.

The pilgrims who slept on the cool marble floors of the mosque were at the mercy of the thousands of Muslims who passed around and over them as they rested. I marveled at the confidence with which they slept and the care that was taken by the passersby not to disturb them. The kindness and mutual respect that I witnessed was overwhelming. I wished the Muslim nation would always be so tolerant and unified.

The birds that flew around the Kaabah were a source of wonder. There were those that flew low and fast over the heads of worshippers as they circumambulated the Kaabah; twice I felt a puff of wind from their wings as they sped past me. And there were those that soared high above the mosque in effortless flight. I wondered at their purpose and their mode of worship, for the Quran says that every kind of creation has its own form of worship.

An account of my pilgrimage would not be complete without a mention of the pain I endured for most of those ten days and many days before the Hajj. A bulging disc and a resulting pinched nerve caused considerable pain in my right shoulder and arm. Sitting and standing for long periods exacerbated the problem, something that cannot be avoided during the Hajj. A veteran of back pain, I prayed for relief and bore it patiently with the belief that whatever happens to a believer is good for him. As the pain worsened, I grew desperate and, feeling totally defeated by pain, I surrendered to what God had chosen for me. I repeated again and again, "Over everything He has decreed. We belong to Him, to Him we are returning, and He can do whatever He likes with us." It was then that I realized that if I could accept pain with faith, then I could accept everything else He has chosen for me: the color of my eyes, the color of my skin, my birthplace, my parents, my siblings, my ailments, my children, my provision, my life span, and my place of death. How many aspects of our lives have we no choice over, yet of which we still disapprove? How can we find faults with what God has chosen for us in His infinite knowledge, wisdom, and love? How do we dare to be ungrateful? Through the pain I realized a valuable lesson in acceptance and trust. It was only then that the pain finally subsided.

Coming home was a challenge. To be a guest in God's house for ten days and to have dedicated and intimate dialogue with Him for this period was a mercy, a comfort and an immense honor. It was a thirst quenched for a brief while. To come home was to replace the shackles of daily life on Earth: distractions, temptations, hard work, fatigue. It took days to muster the resolve I needed to continue living and working to the utmost of my ability with faith in life after death, faith in eternity, and hope for my return to His love and mercy, this time with no end. As I returned to my earthly responsibilities, I prayed, "At Your service, O Lord, at Your service. There is no god but You. All praise, goodness, and authority are Yours. There is no god but You."

The Testimony

La ilaha illa Allah, Muhammad rasool Allah. These words comprise what is known as the *shahada,* or testimony, among Muslims. It is a phrase that is whispered into the ear of a newborn immediately after birth and the words each of us hopes to utter as we pass from this life. I repeat no other words more often, nor are there any more dear to me. What are the meaning and implications of the two parts of the *shahada*?

La ilaha illa Allah. These four Arabic words, which mean, literally, "no god but The God," sum up the primordial doctrine of faith. The meaning of life, the contentment of the soul, and the essence of truth, goodness and justice lie in the understanding of this brief and simple statement. These four words are uttered numerous times a day by every devout Muslim, but their weight is demonstrated in the conversation between Moses and the Lord in this saying of Prophet Muhammad: "When Moses asked God to teach him a prayer to recite whenever he remembered or called upon Him, God answered, 'Say, Moses, "There is no god but Allah."' Moses said, 'O Lord, all of your servants say these words.' God said, 'O Moses, if the seven heavens and all they hold, and the seven earths as well – if all these were weighed against this word of "There is no god but Allah," the latter would outweigh the former.'" To deny the fact that there is only one God, or to believe in a deity beside or other than God, is the single unforgivable sin in Islam. The Quran warns, "Indeed, God does not forgive association with Him but He forgives what is less than that for whom He wills. And he who associates others with God has certainly gone far astray" (4:116). *La ilaha illa Allah.*

God, or *Allah,* is the One Who gives life and brings death, Who owns the Earth and everything on it, Who protects, Who knows the unseen and the visible, and in Whose hand lies control over everything (Quran 23:78-92). Sincerely believing in one God and His omniscience and omnipotence in the workings of the universe gives me clarity, peace of mind and direction for my entire life. Acknowledging that there is no god but He engenders my love for Him, reminds me to call on Him, and prevents me from associating power to any other than God. *La ilaha illa Allah.*

The believer naturally loves God, but the Quran warns against loving others more: "*And yet, among the people are those who take other than God as equals (to Him). They love them as they (should) love God. But those who believe are stronger in love for God...*" (2:165). Therefore, the love for family, friends, wealth, or any object or activity on Earth should not resemble our adoration for God, who is the Giver of such gifts. *La ilaha illa Allah.*

The believer also frequently calls on God, and God alone, because he knows that "*Whoever relies on God will find Him sufficient*" (Quran 65:3). This does not mean that I should not try my best to avoid problems and prepare for a secure future, but I know that God, out of His infinite wisdom and mercy, will facilitate only what is good for me. I am confident that God is always near, hears every prayer, and knows every need. *La ilaha illa Allah.*

It is incumbent upon us to help one another, but the true believer does not rely on others' help before first calling on God's support and doing whatever he can to help himself. The Quran encourages good planning and positive action: "*God will not change the condition of a people until they change what is in themselves*" (13:11). Although I try my best, I never have blind faith in such things as medicine, connections, or my own capabilities, but know that without God's support, nothing can be achieved. I am careful not to give sole credit to other people and things, or believe in luck or superstitions, but acknowledge God's overriding authority and will in every matter. *La ilaha illa Allah.*

Muhammad rasool Allah. The second part of the *shahada* sums up Islamic practice by recognizing Muhammad as the prophet of God, the last of a succession of prophets and messengers that includes Noah, Abraham, Moses, Zachariah, and Jesus, among others. To believe that Muhammad is the messenger of God is to believe not only that he delivered a message from God (i.e., the Quran), but also that he lived according to God's guidance in a way that was approved by Him.

Like the words "I do" said for marriage, *Muhammad rasool Allah* has life-long implications. To believe that Muhammad is the messenger of God is to believe that his commands, prohibitions, characteristics, and habits are also God-inspired. The Quran states, "Accept anything the Messenger may command you, and keep away from anything he forbids you. Heed God; God is stern in punishment!" (59:7) and "You who believe, obey God and His messenger; do not turn away from him after hearing (his commands)" (8:20). God commanded Muhammad to tell his companions, "If you love God, follow me; then God will love you and forgive your offenses. God is Forgiving, Merciful" (3:31). Why wouldn't I follow Muhammad if doing so engenders God's love and forgiveness in return? I am thankful to have a human example of righteousness, or a "human Quran" as he has been called, and I frequently send blessings on Muhammad in appreciation of the hardship he endured to undertake the monumental task of delivering God's message to all mankind.

The *shahada* is a short phrase that, when applied fully over a lifetime, raises us to our highest potential. It assures us that there is a God Who manages the universe purposefully and Who sent a message to us to guide us to both individual and collective success. It provides an example of an upright person, the Prophet Muhammad, who can be followed to gain the Creator's love and forgiveness. If we analyze every problem, question or situation in our lives against the *shahada*, thereafter applying its principles, we will find guidance for every circumstance, peace and contentment on a day-to-day basis, and success that reaches far beyond our earthly expectations – we will inherit Paradise.

La ilaha illa Allah, Muhammad rasool Allah.

Unconditional Love

If love is a sublime and sought-after emotion, then it follows that unconditional love is even more lofty and desired. We seek love because it is enjoyable, affirming, exhilarating. We usually love others for their positive traits – their outlook on life, their ethics and sense of purpose, their enthusiasm and dedication, their honesty and courage, their sensitivity and passion. A lover will compliment their beloveds' beauty, appreciate their virtues, affirm their worth, and enjoy making them happy. But there is much more to love. As Viktor Frankl so eloquently said,

> Love is the only way to grasp another human being in the innermost core of his personality. No one can become fully aware of the very essence of another human being unless he loves him. By his love, he is enabled to see the essential traits and features in the beloved person; and even more, he sees that which is potential in him, which is not yet actualized but yet ought to be actualized. Furthermore, by his love, the loving person enables the beloved person to actualize these potentialities. By making him aware of what he can be and of what he should become, he makes these potentialities come true.[21]

Unconditional love begins when we see others in their totality, the good and the bad. It delights in the good but, although it forgives the bad, it cannot accept complacency. Unconditional love manifests in the presence of vulnerability and imperfection, and is both tested and proven in episodes of confrontation, opposition or rejection. The unconditional lover will risk honesty, which will inevitably hurt you. He wants to make you see, to dare you to new experiences, to open you to change, to push you to the limit of your growth. He wants to uncover what is meaningful and important for your life, what will make you a better person, what will lead you to your ultimate potential. This expression of unconditional love is risky, because not all of us are ready to accept true love. We will often feel hurt, betrayed, painfully *unloved*. In fact, we may avoid unconditional love because it portends discomfort, change, hard work. It challenges us and tires us.

---

21   Frankl, Viktor. *Man's Search for Meaning.*

Love, particularly unconditional love, are gifts to lovers in earthly life, celestial gifts that must have an origin in God. His love for us is evident, and revealed in the gifts of life itself, the physical, mental and emotional capacities we enjoy, the beauty within and around us, and the mystical and spiritual aspirations that lead us to greater awareness of Him. We are naturally inclined to sense God's love and respond to it with gratitude and yearning. We seek God's love and acknowledge it, especially when we are satisfied, pleased. And we yearn for unconditional love, yet we don't understand what it means.

Yes, God is Kind, God is Love. He is Grand, Good, Eternal. He describes Himself as Holy, Compassionate, Merciful. We implore His Gentleness, Generosity, and Forgiveness. We claim to love God. Yes, loving *this* God is easy, and we are willing to love at this level. But God is also Truthful, a Guide who allows distress to afflict His creation, the Lover who sees our potential, who is not satisfied with mediocrity. Are we ready for the Truthful to assess our soul? For the Guide to lead us to and through our vulnerabilities? For the growth envisioned by unconditional Love?

When we are subjected to childhood traumas over which we have no control, when we experience failure and privation despite our best efforts, when we suffer physical pain and material loss in our struggle against injustice, when we are afflicted with natural disasters or life-threatening illness that turn our lives upside down, we blame God, doubting His love. We want love but not unconditional love. We forget that the unconditional lover is not satisfied with the outcome of a pampered life, that which stunts our growth and cripples us. He sees our potential and propels us toward its realization. Sometimes He takes what is unnecessary and distracts us from our purpose. Or perhaps He sees our contradictions and tries to purge our hearts of insincerity. The unconditional lover will forever challenge our status quo, will prompt our growth, and will provide us with the means to flourish.

To perceive and accept unconditional love – that which transforms and elevates you – necessitates a degree of patience and trust. Prophet Muhammad said, "When God loves a people He subjects them to trials, so whoever is content, then for him is pleasure..." The Quran confirms it: *"And We will surely test you with something of fear and hunger and a loss of wealth and lives and fruits, but give good tidings to the patient, who, when disaster strikes them, say, 'Indeed we belong to Allah,' and indeed to Him we will return.' Those are the ones upon whom are blessings from their Lord and mercy. And it is those who are the [rightly] guided"* (2:155-157). If you accept God's unconditional love, you will be vulnerable to Him and accept His will, even that which hurts or perplexes you. Loving unconditionally will make you putty in His Hand, the mighty Hand that shapes you in turn with gentleness and force, with abundance and privation, with that which makes you whole and that which breaks you. He will periodically knock on your heart to crack its fragile shell and give it space to grow. Then, if you meet the tapping with indifference or avoidance, He will insist with greater and greater intensity, until He breaks your hardness and a new heart emerges, pliant in the Hand of its Maker. Are you ready for the unconditional, nurturing love of God in this moment? When He heats you in fire then forges your shape like a blacksmith, will you yield to Him or will you rebuke Him, question His wisdom, rebel against His will?

To love God *conditionally* is to accept His gifts and thank Him when life goes according to plan, but to ignore Him when called, question Him when dismayed, rebuke Him when disappointed, rebel against Him when challenged. To reject God's love is to turn away from and avoid what is good for your soul, what expands and elevates it. To distance yourself from the varying expressions of His love is to become stagnant, numb, and lifeless.

To love God *unconditionally* means to follow Him. It means to love all that is from Him, to seek it, embrace it, and submit to it with total acceptance, without blame. Although loving God will challenge you, and may cause some discomfort from time to time, you won't retreat. You will look beyond any inconvenience, even before the trial of true love begins, and fix your sight on the face of the Beloved. The lover will trust the Beloved with a trust due to none other than Him, saying, "Ask what You will. I am Yours."

Our primordial selves are open to the delights of love. Our mature selves are open to the challenges of unconditional love. With insight, we recognize it when we experience growth after painful or traumatic episodes, and may even be grateful for the truths it revealed or the personal strengths it nurtured. But if we are to move beyond our selfishness on the receiving end of love, and become a lover as well, we must accept the implications of unconditional *loving*—appreciation of how God manifests His unconditional love for us, and then love Him, unconditionally, in return.

We are called to believe in God, to reflect on life, and to comply with His will. The Quran says, *"Whoever believes, it is for his own good and whoever is blind, it is to his own harm"* (6:104) and that the heedless are those who *"have hearts with which they do not understand, and they have eyes with which they do not see, and they have ears with which they do not hear"* (7:179). *"If Allah touches you with hurt, there is none who can remove it but He. If He designs some benefit for you, there is none who can keep back His favor... Truth has reached you from your Lord. Those who receive guidance do so for the good of their own souls and those who stray do so to their own loss... Follow (the Quran that) is revealed to you and be patient and constant..."* (10:107-109).

With our limited knowledge and experience, we can't fully understand God's will, but with complete trust in our Creator, we can accept it, embrace it. When we love God unconditionally, we will seek His guidance and then consciously and faithfully follow it. We will fulfill His prescriptions and avoid His prohibitions. We will be pleased with the Word of God that guides us to our greatest potential and the Hand of God that shapes us into our best selves. We will be able to accept the mysteries of our lives – the unavoidable trauma, pain and want – as being part of the process that makes us who we are, who we were meant to be. We will become resilient to mental, spiritual, and physical challenges, resourceful and strong in the face of adversity, perceptive to others' suffering, compassionate and responsive to their needs, daring against injustice, trusting in ultimate good.

With total submission to a loving and beloved Lord, we can find a place of peace and stability, a place where trauma, pain, and want no longer prevail. We can find a place of love, exquisite in breadth and depth and, if we surrender to it – to the unconditional Love of our Maker – we will be blessed with His pleasure, abundance, and infinite mercy. In our search for this place of love, both in this life and the next, we can only ask God to help us respond to His love with total submission – to offer to our Beloved our own unconditional love.

Breath of Life

Life is a series of breaths, the first being the unexpected inhale and the last being the anxious exhale. But even before we are born into the world, breath defines us. Prophet Muhammad said that when the fetus is 120 days old, a soul is breathed into him, making him suddenly distinct from a mere lump of flesh. God said that our father Adam was fashioned from clay and "then We breathed into him" and he came to life. Our bodies need breath to survive, and that which defines our true selves – our soul – is none less than a breath from God.

I didn't understand the significance of this until 2020. The Covid-19 pandemic fundamentally changed how we communicate, work, socialize, shop and experience the world. For me personally, the lockdown followed retiring from paid employment, leaving my last volunteer position, and living in an empty nest. For months, like many others, I was trapped in my house and, with nowhere to go and nothing to do, I got stuck in my head. I realized it was a mess.

Like junk stacked in corners of a dusty attic, my thoughts needed to be disentangled, examined, sorted. I could have avoided the work ahead because the disarray was tucked away, conveniently ignored, or forgotten. But 2020 sent me deeper and deeper into my mind, where I found many questions. Who am I? Where do I belong? What do I want? What is important, if anything? I didn't like the dark space I occupied but there was no escape. And so I faced the dusty recesses of my mind, forced to process the relics and junk packed away in my mental space.

I experienced a recurring theme in my dreams during this period. It revolved around preparing meals for others, and ended in frustration and failure – burnt or undercooked food, missing ingredients, frantic deadlines, double bookings, unhappy guests. I laughed it off at first. But the final dream in this sequence was the key to one of the boxes marked "childhood." In the dream, I had bought a handful of orphans each a happy meal. But to my dismay, they complained about the taste and nutritional value, and were clearly unhappy with what I thought was a great idea. The dream took me to the memory of cooking meals for my younger siblings. I was ten when my father abandoned us and when my mother took a second job, leaving six kids at home to depend on themselves. Despite my young age, I often cooked for my siblings, dreaming up recipes with the poor quality and limited food staples from the pantry. Suddenly I realized how that experience impacted the next fifty years of my life and that it was time to let it go. I needed to stop blaming myself for things out of my control and for what is not my responsibility to begin with. I needed to remove the burden of accountability for the wellbeing of others from my shoulders and remember what childhood feels like. It would take some time to reconcile my passion for and anxieties about food and hospitality, but at least one box was opened.

Memories from childhood turned into memories of my own children, who have grown and moved away. There was both sadness and relief when I finally admitted to myself that they no longer needed me; in fact, I realized that nobody really needs me. A long-forgotten sense of freedom and possibility surfaced at times, teasing me to consider a fresh start. It was exhilarating to think that my husband and I could embark on a new adventure together. But among the daydreams were those where I was alone. So I had to reassess my roles as wife, mother, and homemaker. Certainly these roles defined me in the past but, like outgrown shoes, they now felt uncomfortable and outdated. Feelings of irrelevance and confinement made me face a question I had to ask and a decision I had to make. In the attic of my mind, I decided to dust off the old photos, frame them and proudly display them, to remind me of what has been important in my life and to inspire me to find new ways to add value to my idea of family. We may not need each other, but we love each other. No adventure, no opportunity, no freedom could replace what I had cultivated over forty years of loving-no-matter-what. I chose my family.

But I knew I needed something more. I've always had many interests and have worked hard most of my life. My last position as associate professor at a teachers' college gradually felt routine, unfulfilling, and futile. Feeling boxed in a job that was never a good fit for my skill set, I retired early. My long-standing volunteer work as manager of an NGO kept me busy for a while, but a shortage of essential support from senior officials made me increasingly discouraged and cynical. I decided to leave and give myself time to figure out what to do next. Having literally nothing to do – apart from daily routines – was difficult because I have always kept myself extremely busy. But the pause was needed. It gave me time to disengage from my professional identity, and space to discover interests from a more genuine place. It was hard to resist the urge to follow the path that my education and experience laid out for me. I had to force myself to stay in the present moment and wait for a question, an interest, a project or a passion to surface. It took months to unearth what I enjoy and to give myself permission to pursue what makes me feel authentic and alive. I know if I commit to developing my passions and answering my calling, work will manifest. But even if it doesn't, the sense of purpose and accomplishment I get from doing the things I love and doing them well will satisfy me. Being authentically me will be enough.

But who is the authentic me? The question, "Who am I?" was the hardest of all. I looked at all the versions of myself packed away in my mind's attic. The ten-year-old homemaker. The troubled teen. The young mother. Wife. Teacher. Volunteer. Grandmother. What defines me? Who was I before I became all that? How does my perception of myself affect how people perceive me and relate to me? What destiny have I made for myself and what power do I have to change it? Who can I become? And, more importantly, who do I *want* to become? I was looking into a mirror, seeing myself but unsure if I knew the person looking back at me. The gaze penetrated my soul and demanded answers. It would not let me turn away.

During this time of soul-searching, I received an email advertising an online course in spiritual healing. Trusting the coincidence and needing some emotional relief, I enrolled. The course mentor, Ihsan,[22] taught about our natural psycho-spiritual state of innocence, joy and love, and the inevitable episodes of trauma that are designed to help us grow emotionally and spiritually. I learned about the effects of un-healed trauma and ways to restore balance, peace and harmony. He encouraged deep breathing, mindfulness and meditation as a way to tap into the Divine Presence, where we can experience true beauty and love. The course helped me in many ways. Most helpful were the guided meditations that urged me to *"remember.... remember who you are..."* It

---

22   https://www.ihsanalexander.com/

was exactly what I had wondered. "*... a servant of the Divine... a Divine breath...*"

All this time I've been searching for God, and I found Him, as close to me as my breath.

And so, before and beyond all my labels, titles, positions, and duties, I remembered my source in God, His breath breathed into my tiny body, and eventually a breath my body will exhale as I make my return journey to my Maker. Now I'm sure of who I am. And now that I know myself, I know everyone. We are all, essentially, a breath from God; we are created by Him, we belong to Him, and we are returning to Him. In the meantime, I will do my best to honor the privilege of my existence and implication of my origin. I will respect myself, and strive to be whole and wholesome, loving and loved, tender and joyful. I will honor all living things, since they, too, house that divine breath. I will stay conscious of my source and my destination and, in between, during this sojourn on earth, I will do my best to stay true to my essence, to always be, first and foremost, a breath of God.

When I leave my bodily dwelling and return to God, I hope that I am recognized as belonging to Him, deemed worthy of His presence, welcomed home at last.

My Pledge[23]

Believing that You have created the universe and all that it contains for a meaningful purpose,

Believing that this present life is temporary, the purpose of which is to test Your creation in their faith and actions,

Believing in life after death, a life which has no end,

Believing in Paradise as a reward for those who win Your favor and in Hell as a punishment for those who incur Your wrath,

Believing that You have endowed mankind with intellect and reason and, furthermore, inspired each soul with knowledge of right and wrong,

> I **Testify** that You are the one and only God, Creator and Master of the universe,
>
> I **Affirm** that my life has meaning and purpose and that my deeds have significance,
>
> I **Vow** to strive in the performance of good deeds not for worldly gain, nor recognition and compensation from fellow men, but for Your sake and in hope of Your acceptance,
>
> I **Promise** to avoid evil of every kind, which is recognizable through both reason and instinct, and
>
> I **Expect** to be rewarded or punished according to my faith and actions.

*

Believing in the Quran, inspired to Muhammad through the angel Gabriel (Jibril), as Your Holy Word, perfectly transmitted, recorded, and preserved since its revelation,

Believing in Muhammad as Your prophet and messenger, the last of a succession of prophets and messengers, who lived according to the Quran and Your inspiration,

> I **Acknowledge** the existence of things unseen: angels, jinn, Satan, the Judgment Day, Paradise and Hell,
>
> I **Accept** the guidance revealed in the Quran and in the speech and actions of your Prophet Muhammad, the obedience of which is binding on me,

---

23   Impressed with a United Nations document, I wrote my personal pledge in its style. -author

I Pledge to fulfill the requirements of faith, namely, to pray the five daily prayers, fast the month of Ramadan, pay alms, and perform pilgrimage to Mecca, and

I Vow to abstain from what You have prohibited.

*

Believing in Adam, who was created from clay, and is the father of all humanity,

Believing in Noah who built the ark and was saved from the deluge,

Believing in Abraham who raised Your House,

Believing in Jacob and his twelve sons, among them Joseph who ruled Egypt,

Believing in David who praised You with the Psalms,

Believing in Moses who parted, by Your Grace, the Red Sea,

Believing in Jesus, born of the Virgin Mary, who was raised to You and who shall come again,

Believing in Muhammad who is Your final prophet, and

Believing in all Your prophets and messengers between Adam and Muhammad,

> **I Bear Witness** that they all are Muslims who believed in your Uniqueness and bowed to Your Will, and that none of them shares in divinity or partnership with You, and
>
> **I Affirm** that I am of their religion as they are of mine.

*

Acknowledging your favors of health, strength, ability and intellect to my person, of sustenance and beauty in my surroundings, of love through family and friends, and of favors that I cannot count and do not perceive,

> **I Thank** You,
>
> **I Pledge** to make honorable use of them,
>
> **I Reject** both miserliness and extravagance regarding their use both for myself and others, and
>
> **I Promise** to share whatever I am granted of your bounties for the benefit of others, be it knowledge, skills, or affluence.

*

Acknowledging Your Absolute Perfection, which is manifested in Your Omniscience, Omnipotence and Supreme Wisdom,

> **I Am Pleased with** what You have chosen for me,

I Trust in Your plan for me, and
I Exercise patience regarding Your Divine Decree.

*

Knowing that You are the Source of peace and security, the Most Gracious and Most Compassionate One, the Healer, the Helper, and the Guide,
    I Seek Your help in all my affairs,
    I Turn to You for solace and relief in times of distress, and
    I Strive to adopt Your attributes in my relations with others, seeking Your countenance only.

*

Knowing that You see and hear all things,
Confirming that every atom's weight of good and evil in me is recorded in Your Book,
Acknowledging my limitations, weaknesses, and forgetfulness,
    I Attest to my own sins committed in thoughts and actions, openly and secretly, intentionally and unintentionally,
    I Beg Your forgiveness, as I try to forgive those who offend me,
    I Depend on Your Guidance, for without it I am certainly doomed, and
    I Plead for Your Mercy, which is my only hope.

THE SEA

I walked on the shore
To gaze at the sea.
Then one still morn
My reflection I saw.
A drop of water!
A miniature ocean
From the great sea of Love.

I inched toward the water
It pulled me in!
I fell, resistance gone
Tumbling, flailing, overcome.
Too much to bear
My flesh immerged
In the ocean of God.

I swam back to the shore
Yet the water was near.
My limbs dripped wet,
The waves I could hear.
Vast, indescribable,
immeasurably sweet,
This love, gift from my Lord.

My soul keeps spilling
This water in me.
Salty tears overflowing
Offered back to the sea.
Immersed in God's presence
I have all that I need,
My love for God, and His for me.

Acknowledgments

Praise be to God who has blessed me in my search for Him and who has enabled me to write about my quest and share it with others. Peace and blessings be upon Prophet Muhammad who was charged with conveying God's message to mankind, and who fulfilled his mission to the extent that his words not only reached me some 1400 years later, but impacted my life in the most profound ways.

I am thankful for the many scholars, authors, speakers and friends who have taught and inspired me over the years. I appreciate the wise editorial advice and suggestions of Hakan Yeşilova at Tughra Books. I am grateful to friends and family for the insight and clarity with which they critically reviewed the text and offered suggestions, among them David Hanners, Norma Tarazi, Tamara Jalving, Maryam Sharak, and Hanah Sharak. I am most indebted to my husband Yaser who has been a guide and support throughout my journey.